THE SUCCESSFUL MANAGER'S ROAD MAP

5 STEPS TO BUILDING A HIGH PERFORMING TEAM

DONNA EVANS

TEAM SUCCESS PUBLISHING COMPANY

teambuildingforsuccess.com

The Successful Manager's Roadmap:
5 Steps to Building a High Performing Team

Copyright 2016

Donna Evans

Published by Team Success Publishing Company
13587 Del Poniente Road
Poway, CA 92064
www.TeamBuildingforSuccess.com

Character and Story Development: Chelsea Hansen
Project Manager: Helen Chang
Editor: Kristine Serio
Copy Editor: Chelsea Hansen
Cover Designer: Gale Spitzley
Illustrations: Stan Evans
Publishing Manager: Laurie Aranda
Publishing Coordinator: Iris Sasing

First edition: 2016

ISBN Numbers: 978-0-9969728-0-2 (softcover)
978-0-9969728-1-9 (hardback)
978-0-9969728-4-0 (ebook)

Library of Congress Number: 2016914578

DEDICATION

To Stan, Ryan and Sarah, for their ongoing
encouragement and support of my endeavors.

And, to the many managers I have known at
Hewlett-Packard and other organizations who strive
to be excellent leaders for their companies <u>and</u>
their employees.

CONTENTS

INTRODUCTION

Congratulations! You have been chosen to be a manager by your organization. You were selected because those in charge believe you have the ability to lead your team to success. You have their vote of confidence, which is a great starting point.

As a manager and leader in your organization, you are in a powerful position in several respects. First, there's the impact to your organization. You are the key link between your company's goals and the employees on your team. Your leadership of your team will harness the abilities and efforts of your employees to achieve important results for your organization.

Second, there's you and your employees. If you successfully manage your team, you set your employees up for success, and also yourself. And you influence the day-to-day quality of everyone's work and personal lives. When your employees go home from work, they'll talk about how much they enjoy working for you. And when you go home, you'll share with friends and family how much you enjoy managing your team.

But you may be asking yourself, how do I become a successful manager? I have found that the most successful managers engage their employees and build high-performance teams. If you can do this, you will be successful. The great news is that, as you build your high-performance team, you'll also grow your own leadership skills so that you're prepared for your next role.

Building a high-performance team may seem like a dream. It sounds good, but it may seem out of reach, even impossible. The purpose of this book is to provide you with a roadmap of five steps you can take to engage your employees and build your high-performance team.

To make this roadmap tangible and relatable, I present the five steps in a fictional story of a new manager, Jeremy, who is struggling with his team and the business. Luckily for him, he meets a mentor, Josephine, who guides him through the five steps to develop a high-performance team in less than a year. As a manager, you may see Jeremy dealing with many of the same problems and situations you face in your role, including poor performance, finger pointing, low commitment and accountability, poor business results, unwanted attrition and tough goals.

If you take the same path as Jeremy, you will realize many of the same improvements Jeremy achieved. Just like Jeremy, though, you need to be intentional in following the steps to build and sustain your team.

Why do I say intentional? You don't automatically become a great manager just because you were promoted into the role. In fact, the transition into the role of manager can be very challenging. You may be managing former peers, or you may have inherited a "problem" team or "problem" employees. Both of these situations are challenging. Also, the skills and knowledge that made you successful as an individual contributor may actually get in the way of your success as a manager. Finally, if you're like many new managers, you have probably found that the demands on your time and energy have gone way up, especially if you're still doing a portion of your previous role.

These can add up to failure for many new managers. The statistics on the failure rate of new managers are staggering. It's estimated that between 50 and 60 percent of new managers fail or underperform in their first two years on the job.

Building a high-performance team doesn't happen overnight. It's a process, and it takes time and energy. This is why I've broken the process down into five steps, with each step creating a foundation for the next step.

The five steps start with you, the manager. First, you will understand how to manage yourself in order to motivate your employees. Second, you must have capable and motivated employees who all know their jobs and the results that are expected and have the support they need from you for success. Third, you and everyone on your team will participate in making sure the team works well together and that everyone has a say in the team's vision, goals, and strategies. Every employee will be committed to doing his or her part for the success of the team. Fourth, the team will develop metrics to ensure the team stays on track, and you will hold yourself, the team, and every employee accountable for achieving the goals of the team. Finally, you and the team will go through renewal to sustain performance for the longer run. The five steps span the full business cycle for a team or even a project.

You may be thinking this will take too long and be too complicated. You can work through the steps fairly quickly. You will need to carry forward the work from earlier steps into later steps. And, you will see an immediate improvement in the functioning of your team by just completing step 1. Your effectiveness in communicating with your employees will improve as you better understand and share information about how you like to work.

The five steps are ongoing. No manager, employee, team, business, or competitive situation is ever the same from one period to the next. You should go through the five steps on an ongoing basis to ensure you're set up for success. I know a number of highly successful business leaders who use many of these same steps and tools annually to maintain and renew their high-performance teams.

At the end of the book, I summarize the five steps, including the outcomes expected from each step. While this story is set in a manufacturing company, the situations and problems could take place in any organization that has challenging goals and poor or inconsistent results.

To gain the most from this book, I suggest you read each step in order and then assess your own situation. You can decide how you want to attack each step. You can try Jeremy's approach or another approach based on your own abilities and situation. You should see an immediate benefit. I'd also recommend you share what you are doing with your employees. Involve them in the solutions and the success of the team. Together, you will create the high-performance team all of you want and need.

THE SITUATION

Monday, January 30

Jeremy's Dilemma

Jeremy listened to the dial tone buzzing through the phone, the all-too-familiar headache creeping up from the base of his skull. Just four weeks ago, on January 4, he'd been promoted to manufacturing manager of All Pro. It had been a big promotion, from senior engineer to manufacturing manager. He'd been so excited that day.

Now, he stared at a picture of Sasha, his wife, on his desk. She stood in the ocean with the sunset throwing orange rays around her frame. Her picture was the only personal item visible in his office. He thought about the call that had just ended with Ben Smith, the procurement manager of Symmetry Technology. Symmetry was All Pro's biggest customer and was located in Silicon Valley, about 180 miles north of All Pro's offices in San Luis Obispo. The call had been very one-sided. Ben had reamed Jeremy out about All Pro's most recent shipment failure. He'd said, "Twenty percent of the parts were defective, and, moreover, that shipment was late. You'd better replace those defective parts by next Friday, or we'll find a supplier who can. You're not the only game in town anymore. We have other options, and we're talking to them."

Jeremy wasn't sure who was involved in the game of "pass the client off until they blow up on whoever picks up the phone next," but it felt like all the blame was his. Jeremy had assured him the parts would be fixed or replaced and that they'd have their good parts by next Friday. Ben abruptly ended the call by saying, "It better be," and hung up without saying good-bye.

Still reeling, Jeremy set the phone down and rummaged some Tylenol out of his top drawer before calling Ken, his boss. The call went to voicemail. Jeremy knew he should tell Ken about the call, but he hung up. He needed to organize his thoughts first. The manufacturing department's performance had been on a downward trend over the last several years, and Jeremy had just been promoted to lead the group. He had assumed he'd be given time to turn manufacturing around. But, given how important Symmetry Technology was to All Pro, it might be the end for Jeremy at All Pro if Symmetry really did go to another supplier. After all, it was his department that had shipped bad parts in a late shipment.

Trying to recover, Jeremy focused on Sasha's picture again. Jeremy had always been fascinated by the way yoga poses seemed to flow from her so naturally. She was attempting to mock cheesy, romantic movies that day on the beach, with her arms spread wide and the water foaming around her calves.

Calmed, Jeremy sent an urgent voicemail to his staff members telling them there'd be a mandatory staff meeting at nine tomorrow morning. He sent an email to Ken telling him about the Symmetry situation and promising they'd have a plan the next morning to replace the parts.

It was late Monday afternoon, and everyone else had left for the day. He sighed and turned his attention to email. His inbox was overflowing, and most of the emails were marked "Urgent." He called Sasha but didn't get a hold of her. He left her an apologetic message saying he'd be working late again and not to expect him for dinner.

The Team in Disarray

Tuesday morning, Jeremy was in the manufacturing conference room fifteen minutes early for his staff meeting. The conference room was just down the hall from his office on the second floor. Similar to Jeremy's office, it was sterile but efficient. It had no windows and a long meeting table that could easily seat fourteen people, more than large enough for Jeremy and his five staff members.

Jeremy was finalizing the agenda on his laptop when Bradley, his production manager, walked in and sat down. Jeremy said, "Good morning." Bradley returned the greeting and promptly opened his laptop.

Bradley didn't engage in small talk. He'd start a conversation only when there was a timely issue or topic. Jeremy heard Bradley sigh and turned around. He saw Bradley scanning his emails.

"Anything wrong?" Jeremy asked.

Bradley replied, "Sean was supposed to send his production plans out by ten yesterday. They still aren't out." He looked up at Jeremy and said, "He's late every other week, and it sets us back."

Jeremy said, "I need to finish these notes. I'll talk to him after this meeting."

The rest of the team walked in except for Sean. Charlie, the quality manager, sat next to Bradley. Anya and Gia, Jeremy's procurement and logistics managers, walked in together and stopped talking. They sat on the other side across from Charlie and Bradley. Jeremy was at the head of the table.

They were so predictable in where they chose to sit. The women would sit on one side and the men on the other. Bradley was still on his laptop, and Gia and Anya were texting on their smartphones. Sean was late. No one was talking to anyone at the table.

This wasn't unusual. Jeremy would usually try to start light discussions with his staff when they first walked in. Sometimes it worked and sometimes it didn't. He didn't even try today. He felt tense himself, given the situation with Symmetry.

Jeremy glanced at his watch. "Let's get started. Sean's late. Gia, since you have your phone out, can you text him to get in here?" Jeremy could feel his blood pressure rising. He shouldn't have to track Sean down. He'd add that to his list of issues to address with Sean.

Jeremy summarized his call with Ben at Symmetry. He concluded by saying, "We can't afford to lose their business. I understand their frustration. Their parts should've been good and on time." There was silence at the table before he added, "I committed to get a replacement shipment to them by next Friday. No later. And the parts need to be good, 100 percent good."

Bradley shook his head. He looked frustrated. "I don't know how we're going to do that. Our production schedule's already full. Do you expect us to rework the bad parts or replace them? If we have to replace them, do we know if we have the materials?" He was looking at Anya.

Jeremy could see that Bradley's tone put Anya on the spot. "I don't know," she abruptly replied. "I just buy the quantity needed for the builds. I don't manage inventory once it's here. Don't you do that?" It sounded more like an accusation than a question.

Glancing at the two, Jeremy saw they were once again going at each other. He said, "Hold on. How do we know if the parts can be fixed or if we'll need to start from scratch?" He looked at Charlie, the quality manager.

Charlie usually looked concerned even when things were going fairly well. Now, he looked totally apprehensive. "I don't know. We'll have to inspect the parts when they come back. Hopefully, we'll be able to fix them with some minor adjustments. But that'll still require the production floor." He added, "I don't know how they got through our quality control when they shipped the first time." He was looking at Bradley.

Instantly, Bradley replied, "We just use the quality system your team sets up. That's all my team can do." He crossed his arms and sat back in his chair.

"Okay," Jeremy said quickly. The finger pointing wasn't new, but it still disappointed him. He ignored it for now given the weight of Symmetry's threat hanging over them. "We need to inspect the parts when they get back to see if they're salvageable. If we need to produce new parts, we'll need to get the new materials in ASAP. And we need to know how defective parts passed our quality tests." He looked around the table. "When will we get the parts back from Symmetry?"

Everyone turned to Gia, the logistics manager. So far, she'd been out of the fray. She said defensively, "I didn't know they were coming. I'll call Symmetry right after this meeting." She made a note on her smartphone.

Jeremy said, "Good. Now, does anyone know why that shipment was late?"

There was silence for several seconds. Finally, Bradley said flatly, "I don't know, but I think it was a combination of things: not enough materials, errors in the production plan, and we had two production stations go down."

No one else said anything. Jeremy was new to manufacturing, so he was still trying to understand how everything worked. Or didn't.

He said, "We've got to get the good parts shipped back to them by next Friday morning, so we'll have to be done no later than Thursday at five o'clock. Let's document who'll do what." He went to the flip chart at the head of the table and listed actions and owners. Then he asked, "Any questions? Does everyone know what they need to do?"

Everyone nodded quietly. There were no questions. Jeremy sighed. It looked like everyone just wanted to get out of the meeting.

Jeremy asked Bradley to stay after the meeting. Sean had never made it to the meeting. Jeremy closed the door. He and Bradley discussed the late production plans from Sean. When Jeremy had first started as the manufacturing manager, he'd talked to Sean about meeting his deadlines and not making errors. He'd assumed Sean would get right on track with a nudge from him because he was the manager. It obviously hadn't worked.

Jeremy thanked Bradley for telling him and said he'd talk to Sean. Jeremy was on edge. He needed to focus on Symmetry and not Sean's poor performance.

Jeremy stopped by Sean's desk. It was down the hall from the conference room. Sean was putting his things away, so Jeremy knew he'd just gotten there. He smiled when he saw Jeremy. Jeremy didn't return Sean's smile and abruptly asked Sean why he hadn't been at the nine o'clock staff meeting. Sean's smile was replaced by a look of surprise. "I didn't know, or I would've been there."

Jeremy felt his frustration level go up. "You should check your email and voicemail every morning, first thing. At least by eight. Got it?" Then, without pausing, he said, "We need to talk. Let's go to the conference room." Once there, Jeremy told Sean about the discussion at the staff meeting. He told Sean to redo the production plans to ensure they could get the replacement shipment to Symmetry on time. Continuing, Jeremy told Sean he could not be late with the plan and that it had to be error free. Sean mumbled it would be. His usually bubbly personality was subdued.

Jeremy said, "Good," and briskly walked by Sean toward his own office down the hall.

Jeremy didn't feel good about the discussion with the team or Sean. He'd let his frustrations with Symmetry flow over into his discussion with Sean. He thought *I hope this job gets easier.*

Jeremy stopped at Ken's office on his way to his own. Ken was busily typing away on his laptop and waved Jeremy in.

Ken glanced at Jeremy and asked, "So, what's the status of Symmetry's shipment?" Jeremy considered sitting down but decided against it so he could make a quick exit if needed.

"They're sending the faulty parts back, should be here tomorrow or Thursday. Our replacement shipment won't have any defects. We should get back on good terms with them." Jeremy tried to be confident.

Ken frowned. "You don't have the parts back yet? And you committed to have a replacement shipment to them next Friday? That seems aggressive."

"I did. We should be able to get it done. They're our top priority."

"Do you know why we shipped defective parts in the first place?"

"Not yet. When we get the parts back, we'll do a complete analysis. Once we figure that out and whether we can fix them or have to replace them, we'll do an inspection on 100 percent of the parts instead of the 10 percent sample inspection we usually do." Knowing Ken's concerns about financials, Jeremy added, "That'll hit our cost of sales."

"Okay. I agree on the 100 percent inspection, but let me know how much your cost overrun's going to be. I'll need to let Richard know." Ken's eyebrows bunched together, and Jeremy saw echoes of the drill sergeant he used to be. The mention of Richard's name caused a knot to form in the pit of Jeremy's stomach. Richard was known for being a brilliant but unpredictable CEO. Jeremy wondered what he'd think of his new manufacturing manager if they lost Symmetry's business.

"I'm not blaming you alone, Jeremy. But manufacturing needs to get its act together. I know you're trying, but this is crucial. We'd be in big trouble without Symmetry. I'm counting on you to fix this. And fast."

This was the closest thing to a pep talk Jeremy had ever received from Ken. Ken gave Jeremy a nod, indicating he was dismissed. Jeremy mumbled a thank you and headed to his desk.

Josephine's Offer

Early Wednesday morning, Jeremy took Sasha to work because her car was in the repair shop. Jeremy had developed a coffee habit when he joined All Pro five years ago. This morning, he wanted a takeout coffee from Roast, the coffee shop that had recently opened next door to Sasha's yoga studio.

"If you see Josephine, tell her I say hi," Sasha said. She kissed him on the cheek and went inside. The name stirred a memory in Jeremy's brain. Did he know Josephine? It wasn't a name you hear every day. Why did it sound familiar?

The smell of coffee bombarded him as he opened the door. He took a few deep breaths. This was Jeremy's second visit to Roast. He enjoyed the calm, warm environment inside that was filled with dark green and burgundy hues, graceful plants, and a beautiful dark wood coffee bar area. The tables and booths were spaced out enough to allow at least some privacy.

When he approached the counter, a petite older woman wearing a burgundy apron over a dark green dress smiled at him from behind the register. The name *Josephine* was embroidered on the lapel.

"You're Josephine? Sasha says hi," Jeremy said. "I'm Jeremy, her husband." She looked familiar, and Jeremy tried to place her.

"Nice to meet you, Jeremy," Josephine said with a slight Southern drawl. "What can I get you?"

"A large nonfat latte."

Jeremy waited to the side and reflected on the previous two days. Everything was harder than it should be: his team, their customers, his workload, his planner, Sean. Ken was a hands-off boss, and Jeremy didn't want to go to Ken and admit he was struggling.

"You look like you need a bigger coffee than this," Josephine said with a warm smile, bringing Jeremy's focus back to the coffee shop. Josephine handed him his coffee. As he was about to say thanks, he realized why she was so familiar.

"You're Josephine," he said lamely.

"Why yes, I am," she said with a slight laugh.

"I mean," he said, stammering, "You're *the* Josephine, the founder of Brilliant Tech. You and your teams were legendary."

"Yes, that's me. I retired from Brilliant Tech, and now I'm just enjoying my coffee shop. And you're a manager at All Pro, right?"

He was surprised she knew that. "Did Sasha tell you?"

"She did."

Jeremy thought of Josephine's career, how she was remembered for her top-notch business results and the overflowing admiration of her employees. She'd been successful at several well-known high-tech companies in Silicon Valley. A wild thought struck Jeremy.

"I know this is crazy. I'm having problems with my team. You've been so successful, and I know your employees loved working for you. I'm wondering how you did all that. Do you have a minute?" Jeremy said in a rush. He was slightly embarrassed about dumping all of that on Josephine with no warning.

Josephine glanced toward the counter, where four employees were taking care of a steady stream of customers. She motioned him toward a booth away from the counter. "Sure. What's going on?"

The question made Jeremy feel dizzy, and he put his coffee down. "A lot, and none of it's good. Our biggest customer is threatening to take their business elsewhere due to quality and delivery problems.

And we have tough goals this year, and I don't know how we're going to meet them. On top of that, my team is struggling. They don't work well together."

Josephine looked at him intently for a few seconds. It felt like she was sizing him up. "Have you managed a team before?"

Jeremy shook his head. "Kind of. I've coordinated some big projects as a senior engineer." He stopped then. "Actually, I've never directly managed people. This is different from managing a project team. I managed tasks and deliverables. Not people. I just went to their managers if I had a problem with somebody not delivering. I didn't have to deal with the people side of it. It's a lot harder than I thought it would be." He paused and said, "I'd heard there were problems. I thought I could fix things."

Josephine looked at him for what seemed like an eternity. "Can I ask why you want to be a manager? Why'd you go after this job?"

Her question caught him off guard. "I thought this would be the next step in my career. I've always been successful. I thought I could be a successful manager too."

"So, you wanted the promotion and everything that goes with it, and you thought it would be easy. Like a promotion from a junior engineer to a senior engineer." Her soft Southern drawl belied her direct, to-the-point questions.

He felt like a kid caught with his hand in the candy jar. "Yeah. I sound kind of shallow, don't I?" He frowned. "I thought I could be a good manager. That it wouldn't be much different from leading a project team."

"Did your boss tell you why they promoted you? Was it because of your project leadership?"

"Yes, exactly. They thought I had the people skills and the task management needed for success."

She smiled. "That's great, Jeremy, and I can see your people skills. Tell me, what would success look like for you and your team?"

He thought for a moment. "Bottom line, we'd win. And it'd be due to great communication and teamwork. My team would do their best and look out for the business. I'd enjoy coming in to work." He paused before adding, "People would go home and talk about how they like working for me. That I'm a good manager."

Josephine smiled and said, "Wow, Jeremy. That's a great vision for where you want to go. You just described a lot of the goals I set for my teams. And believe me, I inherited some dysfunctional teams."

Jeremy perked up. "Really?" he asked.

"You have no idea. And the higher up you go, the more dysfunctional. Tell me about your team. Do you think your employees are incompetent or don't care about the company?"

He considered his team and said, "No, they seem competent in their own areas. Well, I may have a problem with Sean, my planner. Everyone's really defensive. No one wants to be blamed for anything. They seem like they're protecting themselves. And I don't think they even like each other. Some of them at least." He was thinking of Bradley and Anya.

"What about the manufacturing managers before you? How did they manage the group?"

Jeremy thought back to what he'd heard about the two previous managers, Brian and Ted. "Brian was the manager two years ago. I heard he took a hands-off approach. He didn't have many staff meetings. I guess he kinda stayed in his office. Everyone said he managed via emails and spreadsheets. His procurement and logistics managers quit, and he had to replace them. He was fired and replaced by Ted. Ted was in the role about a year. I heard he was hired to get results. Several people told me Ted yelled at his staff and pitted them against each other. Several threatened to quit. His planner did quit and Ted hired Sean, his replacement, about nine months ago. Ted was fired in December."

"It sounds like your predecessors didn't do much to foster teamwork. So, you're their third manager in three years? That's a lot of change."

He shook his head. "Yes, it is. I feel like I walked into a card game with the deck stacked against me."

"You said you had tough goals. How tough are they?"

"We have six goals, and I don't think we're going to hit any of them this quarter. We're way off on quality and on-time delivery to customers."

"How far off?" Josephine asked.

"We're supposed to be at 95 percent quality, and we're at 85 percent. For on -time delivery, we're supposed to be at 90 percent, and we're at 81 percent. We're going to need a huge improvement in February and March to hit our goals. We've been on a downward trend the last several years, and the competition is closing in."

"Those are big gaps." She shook her head and said, "I've been there with teams that are just trending down or stalled out. It's hard to break out of that. Let me ask a question. Would you succeed if all your employees did their best work every day?"

It seemed like a trick question. "Of course. That'd be great. I know we'd win." He looked out the window. "That's not where we are right now though."

She leaned forward and said intently, "You can get there. What it takes is employee engagement. When employees are fully engaged, you can achieve great things." She was energized now.

"I've read about employee engagement, but it sounds like consultant speak."

"Believe me, it isn't just consultant speak. If you can effectively engage your employees in the business and build a united team, you'll be successful. You've probably seen that with teams you've been on before."

He thought about her description and remembered his first engineering job, at XFactor. His first team had been very dynamic, and everyone had pitched in to make the group successful. He smiled and said, "Yes, I have. It was a really fun group to be part of. We worked so hard, but we always delivered."

She must have seen his reaction. "You know what I'm talking about."

Thinking about his current situation brought him back to reality. "I need to turn this around, and quick. I don't feel like I have much time."

"The good news is you're still in the honeymoon phase with your team. But that's gonna end soon. You can make good progress quickly if you work at it. But you have to be intentional."

"Intentional?" Jeremy asked. "I'm not sure I know what you mean or what I'd do."

She glanced at the counter.

"I'm sorry if I'm taking too much of your time."

"We're fine. My team's taking care of it." She turned back toward Jeremy. "Building any good team takes effort and work. It's a process. You've heard that before, I bet." Then she laughed.

"Sure. I get that, I guess." He wasn't sure where the conversation was going.

She went on. "I break it down into five steps. I go through the five steps every year with myself and my team because change is ongoing. Even here." She was looking around Roast.

He looked around and remarked, "Roast certainly looks like it's working."

"Thanks, Jeremy. I like to think so. But let me show you something." She took a napkin and drew five circles, connecting them into a ring.

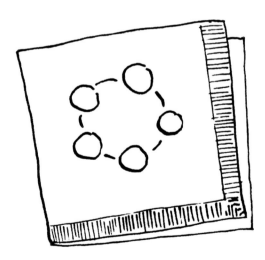

"The five steps are related, and the first provides the foundation for the next and so on. If you want to achieve your vision of your great team, I'll work through the five steps with you. But, before you decide whether you want my help, think about what I said." She smiled as she got up from the booth. "I hope you're willing. I've got to go, and you probably need to get to work. Let me know."

Surprised by her offer, he could only muster an "okay" as she walked away. He wasn't sure she heard him.

He picked up the napkin. His feelings were mixed. On the one hand, he felt a little awestruck from having the legendary Josephine offer to help him. On the other hand, he worried that he'd fail and need to find a new job. Would Sasha have to give up her yoga studio and go back to the corporate world? Would they have to move so he could find another job? They'd escaped hectic Silicon Valley four years ago and loved the San Luis Obispo area. He sighed.

Looking at the napkin, he liked the fact that she had the five steps. At least that was logical and orderly. He put it in his pocket. He wanted to think about it more, but now he needed to get to work. He faced another long day.

Sasha's Advice

Later that night, while cooking dinner with Sasha, Jeremy shared his frustrations with work. Then, he told her about his unanticipated discussion with Josephine that morning. He showed her the napkin with Josephine's five circles. She paused in stirring the spaghetti sauce to look at it.

"Why are all the circles blank?" she asked.

"We didn't have time to fill them in. She said to come back if I decide I want to do the five steps." He shifted the garlic bread around on the baking sheet and said, "She said I'd be able to engage my employees and harness their power with the five steps. I don't know if I have time to do five steps."

"Do you think you'll get fired if you keep having problems?"

"That's what happened to the last two manufacturing managers." He set a plate by the oven for the bread. "I know we've been talking about buying a house. And maybe starting a family. It wouldn't be a good time to get fired."

She continued to stir the sauce. "Well, it would be disappointing. Especially if we'd have to move. My yoga practice is just starting to take off." Then she smiled at him, saying, "It wouldn't be the end of the world, though. I think you should work with Josephine. You said she has a great reputation, and there is something about her that's . . ." She paused, searching for the right word. "Different. She seems so competent. I think she can help you with your team. It seems like your team has a lot of problems."

"They're a big part of it. They just don't get along. It feels like there's tension with the group. Finger pointing and comments that are negative," he said.

"Do you know why?" she asked.

"I think it's a lot of things. The previous two managers weren't effective. And the people on my team are diverse in so many ways. I think they all have different ethnicities. Gia is Indian, I think. Bradley is African-American. Anya has that classic Scandinavian look. I think Charlie is Jewish. Then, there's a generational thing going on. I've probably got Baby Boomers with Bradley and Charlie. I'm not sure exactly how old they are. But they make comments about how the others don't do their jobs and that they're always on their phones.

"Anya may be a Gen Xer. Gia and Sean are Millennials. Those three are kind of new to All Pro, so they don't have the experience Charlie and Bradley do. And that causes issues too," he added.

"I could see that," Sasha said.

"And their personalities couldn't be more different. Anya and Bradley just seem to grate on each other. Bradley's quiet and very organized. He's been the glue keeping everything together. Anya's so outgoing but kind of all over the map. She just says whatever she's thinking. And it bugs Bradley." He sighed. "She also has a young child and has to leave by five. Bradley doesn't say anything, but I can tell that bothers him. He takes pride in how many hours he's at work. He puts in more than I do."

Her expression changed to a look of disapproval. "I think you put in too many hours as is. I hope that's not going to continue. I like having dinner together."

Jeremy put his arms around her waist and said, "I like having dinner at home too. I can't promise I'll be home every night for dinner, but I'm working on it."

"Good." She gave him a quick kiss on his cheek as she walked over to the table. "It's too bad you can't get the best from everybody. You'd have a great combination."

"You're right. Except maybe for Sean. I'm not sure Sean is cut out to be a planner. He makes so many mistakes, and it seems like he's not learning from them."

"That doesn't sound good." She poured the pasta into a strainer and said, "Well, you said Josephine talked about employee engagement. I've seen a few articles about it, and it sounds like a good idea." She took the pasta to the table. "Let's eat."

Later, he looked up employee engagement online. He decided there was a lot he could buy into. He found studies from organizations such as Gallup that documented the business ROI of higher employee engagement.

Jeremy Buys In, and the Bad Parts Are Back

Thursday morning, Jeremy found the napkin still sitting on the counter. He looked at the five circles for a moment and then put the napkin in his pocket.

On his way to work, he stopped by Roast to try to catch Josephine. He ordered a double latte to go and then asked the barista, "Is Josephine here?" The barista disappeared into a back room and reappeared with Josephine at his side.

When she saw Jeremy, a huge smile appeared. "Good morning, Jeremy."

Jeremy pulled the carefully folded napkin out of his pocket and slid it across the counter. "Good morning. I want to fill these in." He paused. "Can you help me? I really need your guidance."

She said, "I'd love to. Can you meet me here at 6:30 tomorrow morning?"

He was relieved. "Definitely. I'll be here."

"Great. Bring a notebook with you. I have to run. Oh, and it looks like your coffee's ready." She pointed to the pickup area where a cup was waiting. Then, she promptly turned and walked toward the back of the shop.

Jeremy picked up his coffee and walked to his car, feeling a little better about his situation. Then he drove to work, hoping the parts would be back from Symmetry.

When Jeremy walked in to work, he went directly to the production line. There was no sign of the returned parts. Instead, he saw normal production work taking place. He caught Bradley as he was walking toward the production line.

"Are the Symmetry parts back yet?" Jeremy asked.

Bradley replied briskly, "I don't know. We're busting our butts to get our other orders out early. I expect Gia's team to give me a call when they arrive." He clearly wanted to get back to the line.

"I appreciate your work to get our other orders out on time, but Symmetry is critical," Jeremy replied.

"I know, but it's Gia's job to manage and move materials that arrive on site."

Bradley seemed on edge, so Jeremy didn't want to push him. Instead, he said, "I'll go over to receiving and check."

Jeremy didn't see the returned parts as he walked through the receiving area to Gia's office, though it was packed with boxes and pallets of parts so it was possible he had missed them. She was putting her laptop on her desk when Jeremy walked in.

"Good morning," Jeremy said. "Did the Symmetry parts arrive?"

Smiling, she said, "Let's check."

They walked to one of her leads, Gary, who was reviewing notes on an iPad. "Have we received a shipment from Symmetry Technology?" she asked.

A quizzical look appeared. "From Symmetry? Don't we usually ship to them?"

Gia explained the situation. Gary said, "No, but I don't know where we're going to put them when they arrive." He glanced around. "We're really tight on space."

Nodding in agreement, she said, "Once you receive them in, just take them over to the production line."

Gary said, "Okay."

As Jeremy and Gia headed back toward her office, he asked, "Can you follow up with Symmetry and the shipper on when the parts will arrive?"

"Okay, I will, but they aren't great on returning my calls," she said.

Jeremy felt his frustration increase. "We need to find out when they'll arrive. Keep calling. I'd like an answer by nine. If you can't find someone, I'll call their procurement manager to get an answer."

He turned to walk away and then remembered his discussion with Bradley. "Can you also talk to Bradley about moving the returned parts to the production area when they arrive? He's trying to get ahead on other orders, so he doesn't have a lot of space, either."

She rolled her eyes and said, "I will. He's not going to be happy. He's so picky about his space, but I'm full up like Gary said."

Jeremy ignored the fact that she'd rolled her eyes. He needed to get back to his desk for a meeting with Ken. "He'll want to know before you just move the parts in, so please ask him."

As he walked away, he thought about Bradley and Gia. They were so focused on just their jobs and not talking to each other.

Thankfully, the parts arrived shortly after noon and were moved to the production area. Bradley and Charlie's teams began the tedious job of inspecting the parts. They'd be working late Thursday, Friday, and maybe into the weekend to sort good from bad parts and figure out what had caused the defects.

OVERVIEW OF THE FIVE STEPS

Friday, February 3

Josephine Introduces Jeremy to the Five Steps

Josephine and Jeremy sat down to begin their early morning meeting. Roast was still quiet. Jeremy had a quizzical look on his face. "Thank you so much for working with me," he said. "Can I ask you a question?"

She nodded. "Of course."

"I'm wondering why you'd do this. You know, help me."

"Good question. I enjoy it, bottom line. I like working with others who aspire to be good managers. Especially with new managers who have the right goals." She paused for a moment. "Jeremy, to be honest with you, I didn't have to open Roast, either. But I have the luxury of time and money, so I can choose how I spend my time. Okay?" she asked.

He nodded and opened his notebook.

She said, "Let's get started on the five steps by filling in the circles." She took the notebook and drew five circles, starting with one at the top and moving clockwise. She connected the circles with a line and then spun the notebook around for him to see.

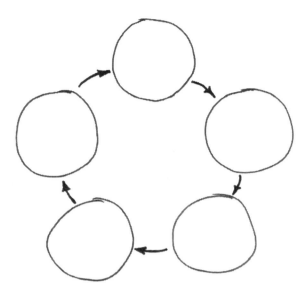

"Let's go through the steps," she said. "You can fill in the circles. In the first circle at the top, write '1' and then 'Embrace Your Role as a Manager.' Being an effective manager is challenging. In step 1, you'll understand your role and your transition into the role. You'll also think about strengths and weaknesses, especially around communication and forming effective relationships with your employees. You'll use that information to be effective in step 2."

Jeremy started taking notes.

She continued with the steps. "Step 2 is 'Engage the Employees.' In step 2, you get the right employees on board. You'll also make sure everyone knows who's doing what and what the expectations are. You'll get agreement with each of your employees on what you can do to help them be successful."

Jeremy interrupted her. "You said 'right employees,' correct?"

"Yes. Having good employees with the right skill sets and right motivations is key to your success. Why do you ask?"

"Sean, my planner, is struggling. It's really causing problems for the rest of my team."

"It's always good to deal with performance problems right away. Do you want to talk about him now?"

"No, not now." He didn't want to go into it today. "Let's go on and finish the steps."

"Okay. Step 3 is 'Build Commitment and Accountability to the Team and the Business.' You'll build trust in the team and you'll engage the team in the business so they're committed to its success. Each employee will know the team's goals."

Jeremy looked up from his notebook, where he'd been filling in the five circles. "They know the team's goals." He felt a little sheepish when he realized he probably sounded defensive.

She smiled. "They know them, which is great. But have they internalized them as their goals? Do they take personal responsibility and ownership for all the team's goals?"

He nodded his head up and down. "You're probably right. I'd love to get that total ownership. Right now, it feels like it's all on me."

"Exactly. You get it." Then she continued, "Step 4 is 'Deliver Results.' You'll manage execution to achieve your goals. You and your team will know where you stand on achieving your goals, and you'll make course corrections. Performance management and feedback are key in this step to make sure the team stays on track."

When she said "feedback," Jeremy felt his anxiety level go up. He was staring at the fourth circle and tapping his pen on the notebook.

"You're tapping your pen. What's up?"

He looked up and said, "Performance management and feedback. I don't like giving feedback, and I thought performance management means firing people."

"That's what most people assume. Performance management and feedback are intended to make everyone and the business successful. With a heavy, heavy emphasis on the positive. Sometimes you do need to address performance that's off track, but that shouldn't be required too often if you've done the first three steps."

"I'd like to see that happen."

"It makes all the difference in the world." She sounded so matter of fact that Jeremy dropped it.

He continued, "If that's step 4, what's step 5, then? It seems like getting results would be the last step."

"Step 5 is 'Renewal.' You have to go through renewal to sustain a high level of performance. Step 5 is about renewing yourself and your team for the long haul. You'll assess the past so you learn from it. And you'll celebrate accomplishments and recognize growth. It'll give you a springboard for your next cycle through the five steps."

She paused and sat back. "Well, now that we've walked through them, what do you think?"

Jeremy looked at his notes. "It all makes sense. I just wonder if it'll work for this team. And how long it'll take. I don't feel like I've got much time to turn it around."

"It's always worked for me. I use it here at Roast," she said, looking around. "If you take your team through the five steps, you'll get improvement, and it can happen quickly. There is a method and process involved. For my own purposes, I broke it into chunks. That's why there are five steps. You can do the steps as quickly as you need to. The other thing is that you'll get an immediate benefit when you start with step 1."

"How would that work?" he asked. It seemed too good to be true.

"One of the immediate outcomes from step 1 will be better communication with your employees and the team overall. That assumes you carry what you learn from step 1 forward with you. And step 2 and so forth. Make sense?"

"That sounds good. Thanks for explaining." He needed some immediate progress.

She paused for a moment. "I've just found it easier to eat in small bites. Just like the muffin I'm going to grab." She smiled and left Jeremy alone for a minute.

When she returned, he asked, "Can we start on step 1 now?"

"You bet. Let's start eating." She put the pumpkin spice muffin down between them and gave Jeremy a fork.

Embrace Your Role as a Manager

Friday, February 3

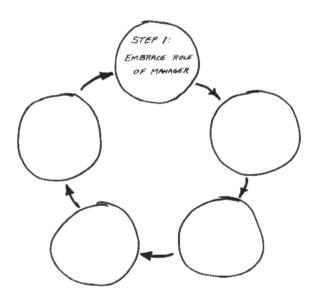

Jeremy's Transition to Management

They started on the muffin and continued their meeting. Josephine asked Jeremy, "How are you doing on Symmetry's parts?"

He finished a bite. "We got the parts back yesterday afternoon, so Bradley and Charlie's teams are sorting good parts from bad. They're analyzing bad parts now."

"And how's the team handling that?"

"Well, it's a little frustrating. I feel like I almost have to play referee between some of my staff members. They seem like they're stuck in their silos." He told her about his discussions with Bradley and Gia, and then he picked up his pen, ready to start step 1.

Josephine asked, "Before we start step 1, did you follow up on the comments Bradley made or Gia rolling her eyes?"

He thought back to those discussions. "With Bradley, no. I really wanted to find out where the parts were. With Gia, I thought about it, but I was late for a meeting with Ken." He realized he sounded defensive. "I guess I should have, huh?"

"I think so. You could have asked Bradley how he was doing because he seemed on edge. And you could have asked Gia why she rolled her eyes. Were you feeling under a lot of pressure yourself? Or you did you not want to have those conversations?"

Sighing, he admitted, "It's probably a bit of both. I tend to avoid conflict. And, yes, I'm feeling under a lot of pressure to get those parts back to Symmetry on time. I've got ultimate responsibility for manufacturing's results."

She smiled. "You do. On not wanting to be involved in difficult or emotional conversations, I hope you know a lot of managers feel that way. Most, like you, take the easy path and don't deal with it. But it's part of the job."

He tried to smile. "Well, it's good to know it's not just me."

"Can I use your notebook and pen for a minute?"

"Sure." He handed them to her.

"Let's talk about your role as a manager." Turning to a blank page, she wrote "Company Goals" and "Symmetry's Demands" on the right side of the page. On the left side, she drew two stick figures. She pointed to the right side of the page. "You have the company's goals over here, including turning around this Symmetry shipment." Then she pointed to the stick figures on the left. "And then you have your employees over here. You'll have to excuse my drawings. I never got past stick figures in my art classes."

Jeremy laughed and said, "Mine look like robots."

"Your job is to get these employees on the left to do their best work so you achieve these company goals on the right."

She drew another stick figure in the middle of the page. "This is you." She wrote "Jeremy" next to the stick figure.

Looking at her sketch, Jeremy said, "I completely get that. I feel caught in the middle, and I don't feel like I have control over either end: my deliverables or my employees."

"Exactly. You don't have control." She pointed again at the stick figure employees. "You've been here, one of these employees. You probably didn't have control over the goals you were given, but you did control your own work. Now, you're in the middle. Your job is more like the role of a conductor for an orchestra." Pointing again at the employees, she said, "You don't make the music anymore. You've got to get your employees to make it. Beautiful, harmonious music so your team delivers the company's goals. If they're successful, you'll be successful." She looked expectantly at Jeremy. "And being a good conductor requires using different skills and a different approach than being a great soloist. Well, in your case, a great engineer."

He was looking at her drawing of him in the middle. "I'm not sure I'm cut out to be a conductor. And, I have to admit, I like having control. At times, I feel like I'm herding cats."

She had a twinkle in her eye. "The one person you do have control over is you. And, you can have a profound influence on your employees. On the quality of their day-to-day work life. And on All Pro's success."

She'd thrown down the gauntlet. He wanted to make a difference, to have that positive impact.

"The question is whether you're willing to really step into the conductor or manager role. It's challenging. I like to think about the role of the manager as having two very different halves that are tightly bound. One half is the work or task side. Some people call it managing the head. The other is the people half. Some people call it managing the heart. But you have to manage both halves. And they're so different. The task half is about organizing the work so it's orderly and trackable.

Like the project management work you did. The people half involves dealing with people and their personalities and emotions. Have you heard of Dale Carnegie?"

"Yes, wasn't he a famous speaker a while back?"

"Yes. And one of my favorite quotes was from him. He said, 'When dealing with people, remember you are not dealing with creatures of logic, but creatures of emotion.'"

He grinned in appreciation. "Sometimes, I do wish I could just deal with robots. Life would be a lot easier."

She laughed. "Sometimes I feel like that too. Now, most managers have a bias in how they manage. They're more comfortable managing the people side versus tasks or vice versa. It's based on their own strengths and weaknesses."

Pausing for a moment, she looked at him with an encouraging smile. "An important part of step 1 is understanding your strengths and weaknesses. What do you think your biggest strengths are?" she asked.

He thought about what had made him successful in his previous jobs. "I'm very results and detail oriented. I'm good at analyzing data and problems and coming up with solutions. I like setting up processes and being efficient. Those all helped me be a good engineer. I got a lot of good work done."

"I can see that," she said. "Now, what about your weaknesses?"

He thought about situations he had found challenging. "Sometimes I can be abrupt with people because I want to get to results. And I don't always listen very well because I want to get to a solution. I don't like it when people get emotional. And I don't do small talk very well. I'm not a really social person. Sasha teases me that, when I go to a party, I can track down engineers like I'm a bloodhound and I'll talk to them the whole time."

"That's too funny. I love that description. That sounds like my husband. Your descriptions would say that you really feel more comfortable with managing tasks versus people. That sounds right based on what you said happened in your discussions with Bradley and Gia."

"Yep. You're right."

"Because you're so task and results focused, that's where you direct your time and energy. I'm not going to tell you that it's not important to manage tasks and results. But, as a conductor, you'll also need to create an environment where your employees and the whole team are motivated to do their best work. When are you motivated to do your best work?"

He thought about her question. "It's probably a combination of things. When I know my work and opinions are valued. When I'm working on something important and I know I'm making a difference." He paused, "And especially when I can trust my boss and people I work with."

She smile, "That's what I've found too. People will be much more motivated if they trust you and believe you care about them."

What she said made him think. He whole-heartedly believed in trust, but *caring* he asked himself?

She must have seen his reaction. She said with a grin, "Does caring about people seem too touchy feely?"

"Well, I do care about my people and how they're doing. It's just I hadn't framed it in my mind that way."

"I believe you care about your people. Men tend to not think of it that way. As you work to build trust, your people will come to see that you care."

"Okay. How do I make that happen? I need concrete ideas."

She grinned. "You're such the engineer." Then her expression became serious. "But you're facing a bigger hurdle because of your two predecessors. You've been their manager only what, a month?"

"Yes. I started January 4."

"Focus on building trust with your employees. You'll need to invest time and some energy to do that. Let me ask, do you have regular meetings with each of your employees?"

"Not yet. It's been hectic. Of course, I meet with them when there's an issue. A need."

"Even in those meetings, check in with your employees on how they're doing. Especially if you sense somebody is concerned or stressed. Like with Bradley. Or follow up if you question what they're doing, like rolling their eyes. Lean into it and ask if there's anything you can help with. It won't add that much time to your meetings, and you'll find out what they're thinking or are concerned about. Until you ask, you won't know. The other plus is that asking will let them know you're concerned about them. That you care."

"What if I need to correct what they're doing? If it's bad for the team? Like with Gia, if she's always rolling her eyes."

"Tell her you saw her roll her eyes. Ask her if she knows she does it. She may not even be aware that she does. Give her a chance to explain. She may think she has a valid reason. You should explain that it has a negative effect on others, including you. Ask her to stop. Make sure you tell her why it's bad for the team. And most importantly, tell her you value what she brings to the team."

Jeremy was scribbling notes down and said, "That helps. I've never been keen on those types of discussions, but I think I can with that approach."

"Good. So, let's talk about having regular one-on-one meetings with each of your employees," she said.

He was beginning to feel overwhelmed. "Things are so hectic, I don't know if I have time for those types of meetings with every employee in addition to my other meetings."

"Now, Jeremy, is that really the case, or is that your bias toward action showing up?"

Yikes. Even when delivered in a soft Southern drawl, what she said hit him like a cold wave. After a moment, he said, "I've never thought of my bias toward results as creating problems."

"It may not be obvious, but taking the time to meet one on one will result in better relationships with your employees, and it'll save you time in the long run. As they get to know you, they'll trust you. If they trust you, they'll bring up issues you otherwise wouldn't hear about until it's too late."

She had him. He thought about his great relationship with Sasha. He trusted her implicitly, and he was sure she felt the same way. "You're right. Life is easier with trust."

She nodded knowingly. "Yep. For me too."

He wrote down more notes.

She added, "Each employee will have different approaches and different needs. It might be good to think about who's more task oriented versus people oriented."

"That's a good idea. I'm pretty sure Bradley is task oriented and Anya is people oriented. I'll have to think about the others." He was starting to list his employees in his notebook.

She said, "Just remember, even task-oriented people like to feel cared about." Then she smiled.

He chuckled. "Yes, we do. I'll schedule those one-on-one meetings. What about motivating the whole team? I have some big team issues."

Nodding her head, she said, "I like to share information with the whole team at once. For example, I share my strengths and weaknesses with my whole team and how I like to work. When I opened Roast, I told them my strengths are starting conversations with anybody, being enthusiastic, and bringing a lot of energy to work. I also told them one of my biggest weaknesses is that I'm not very organized. I asked them to pin me down on details and to let me know if they think I'm missing something."

Jeremy laughed. "I can see it helps me know you and what I need to do to get what I need. But with my team, I'm not sure I want to share my weaknesses. Won't that make me look like a weak manager?"

"No, it actually lets people know you're human and what they should expect. They'll trust you more if you're vulnerable with them. If you open up with them, they'll open up with you."

He added notes to his notebook and asked, "What else would you recommend?"

"Share your goals for the team. Like what you told me the first time we met. You said you wanted teamwork and great results and so forth. You should share that with them. It gives them hope for the future and insight into you, and it also helps set a tone for the team."

"That's a good idea." He looked at his lengthy notes from their discussion. "I have quite a list."

She said, "That's probably enough for today."

"Yes. This has been great. I feel like I have a path forward."

"Good. I accomplished my mission."

They parted ways after scheduling another 6:30 a.m. meeting for the next Tuesday. Jeremy had a lot to get done once he left Roast. He was glad it was Friday. He was looking forward to spending the weekend with Sasha. And thinking about what Josephine had said.

Deciding What He'll Change

Jeremy's weekend started off well. He and Sasha went on a dinner and movie date Friday night. Sasha had persuaded him to see a chick flick. It wouldn't have been his first choice, but it turned out to be a romantic comedy, and he enjoyed it.

His Saturday morning started off the usual way. Sasha left at eight to teach a yoga class. Jeremy started his list of chores, but he kept thinking about his discussion with Josephine. His chores could wait.

He sat down and reviewed his notes. First, he listed his strengths. He needed to make sure he used his strengths when warranted. The strengths that stood out the most were his focus on efficiency and results. If efficiency was overused, he might not take the time to recognize his employees or get to know them better. If his focus on results was overused, he might overlook poor behavior.

He thought about what he'd do differently this next week. He'd start by changing his usual daily routine. He'd go out of his way to talk to his employees. He knew everyone would be under the gun to get the Symmetry parts shipped out by the end of the day on Thursday. He'd schedule a special staff meeting on Friday to thank his staff for fixing the parts by the deadline. Then, he'd do as Josephine suggested and share his goals and his strengths and weaknesses with his team. He'd tell them about the regular one-on-one meetings he'd have with each of them starting the next week.

The one area he was concerned about was leaning into conflict and emotions. Josephine made it sound easy, but he wasn't sure he'd be able to do it in the moment, when it was most needed. He'd have to think about that over the weekend.

He felt better about following up on Josephine's coaching. He left his notebook open on the kitchen counter when he went out to clean the rain gutters.

Sasha was home by one o'clock. She was reading his notebook when he walked in from mowing the lawn. "What's this?" she asked. Jeremy told her about the discussion with Josephine and his plan for implementing her recommendations.

"It sounds like a great discussion and plan."

He replied, "There's one thing I'm trying to figure out still. I know it's an issue for me."

"What's that?"

"I'm not sure I can deal with conflict, in the moment. Like, lean into it." Then, he told her about Gia rolling her eyes when she talked about Bradley. "I took the easy way out and didn't deal with it."

Sasha smiled. "Can I tell you how I try to handle those situations? I don't always do it, but I'm getting better."

"Definitely." He often found her ideas helpful because she thought about things differently from how he did.

She said, "I take a deep breath and try to pause before I do anything. That gives me just a moment to think about it. I can choose how I'm going to respond."

"Hmmm, that's interesting. So, like with Bradley, I noticed his frustration. Instead of just going to my next task, I could've paused and thought about what I was seeing. I'm going to try it out." He gave her a quick kiss on the cheek. "Thanks. You're really good at stuff like that. You're so calm."

She laughed. "I don't always feel calm. But I do find pausing before I react really helps."

He added that to his notes. He felt better about that part of the upcoming week.

He knew Bradley, Charlie, and many of their employees were working over the weekend to inspect the faulty Symmetry parts. He stopped by work Saturday afternoon. They were making good progress, but it was too early for any conclusions.

Connecting with His Employees

Early Monday morning, Jeremy parked his old Toyota Camry in one of the parking spots close to All Pro's two-story building. He saw Bradley's Ford F150 pickup in the lot. Instead of going directly to his desk, like he'd normally do, Jeremy stopped by Bradley's desk, which was right by the production floor on the first level. His back was turned to Jeremy, and he was talking to one of his production associates. He was just finishing when Jeremy walked up. Bradley looked surprised to see Jeremy. "You're in early."

Jeremy grinned. "I know we've got a lot going on, so I want an early start. How are things going?"

Bradley quickly reviewed the work that his production group and Charlie's team had finished on Sunday. They had discovered that one of the components in the parts had been slightly modified by the supplier, which had caused the defect in the parts shipped to Symmetry. Their quality control process hadn't caught it.

Jeremy could sense Bradley's frustration. Remembering Josephine and Sasha's advice, he paused and then said, "It looks like you're frustrated."

Bradley emphatically responded, "You bet I am. Anya and her buyers aren't staying on top of her suppliers. You know, this isn't the first time I've had to clean up after them. Do you know how many hours we put in from Thursday to yesterday?"

Jeremy nodded. "I know it's a lot. And I know we have a busy week ahead of us too. Thanks for sorting through all those parts and getting down to the cause. I'll follow up with Anya to see what she knows about the change and how the change happened. We should have re-qualified the part."

Bradley seemed a little calmer. "Yes, that would have saved us all of this." He was gesturing toward pallets of sorted parts.

Jeremy said, "I've scheduled a staff meeting at nine this morning to discuss the results and our next steps. We need a game plan to turn the shipment around by end of day Thursday."

Bradley said he'd be there and turned to walk back to the production line.

Jeremy quickly called out Bradley's name. Bradley turned around. Jeremy said, "Thanks again for all the work over the weekend. And thank your team too. Can I can bring pizza in for your team?"

Bradley was clearly surprised, and his face seemed to soften. "I'll check with the group." Then, he continued walking to the line.

Jeremy was glad he'd come in early and talked to Bradley. Before his discussion with Josephine, he would have just gone to his desk and sent an email to Bradley.

Jeremy went to his office on the second floor and left urgent emails and voicemails for his team, telling them about the mandatory meeting at nine.

Jeremy made a point of stopping by Anya's desk a few minutes early on his way to the meeting. He wanted to give her a heads up on the inspection results and check on the faulty component. She was just putting her purse away in her desk when Jeremy walked up.

He said, "Good morning," as he came to the doorway. She looked surprised and harried. Jeremy rarely stopped by her desk.

"Oh. Hi, Jeremy. I know about the meeting." She sounded a bit defensive.

Remembering Josephine's advice, he asked, "Did you have a good weekend?"

She gave him another surprised look. "Uh, it was okay. Noah, my son, was sick, so that wasn't great. I had to run him to my mom's house this morning because he can't go to day care. So I'm feeling a bit scrambled right now."

Jeremy knew she had a son but not much else. "I hope he gets better soon."

She smiled. "Thanks. Me too."

Jeremy then told her about the weekend inspection results and the faulty component from the supplier. He asked, "Did you know about the change by the supplier?"

A look of disappointment crossed her face. "No, I didn't, but that part's being managed by a new buyer. I'll check with her ASAP and find out what she knows."

Jeremy thanked her, and they walked down the hall to the conference room.

Everyone else, including Sean, was already there at nine when they walked in. Jeremy thanked everyone for being on time. He wanted to begin the meeting on a positive note, so he started by thanking Charlie and Bradley for their hard work over the weekend. Then, he asked them to report on what they had found. They concluded their report by saying they could fix the bad parts by running a second shift on the line starting Wednesday morning. But they'd have to get good components from the supplier by the end of the day on Tuesday.

Gia asked why the parts were defective. Bradley immediately turned to Anya and asked pointedly why the supplier had changed the part. She retorted that she had just now found out about the change and was following up with the buyer. She adamantly said, "We'll get the replacement components by end of the day Tuesday." An alarm went off in Jeremy's head when he heard Bradley's pointed question and Anya's strong reply. He took a deep breath and paused before saying, "This is a stressful situation, but I know everyone's doing their best to turn this around. Let's focus on what we can do to fix the situation."

They continued to work through the details of getting good parts back to Symmetry by Friday. Jeremy concluded the meeting and finished up a note on his laptop. Anya hung back and, after everyone else left, said, "Thanks, Jeremy, for the heads up on the part. At least I was ready for Bradley's question."

Jeremy said, "You're welcome. Let me know too if you want help on the discussions with that supplier. I know the head of engineering there."

She replied, a little surprised, "Thanks, Jeremy. I might do that. I've been in this role for a year, and it's been harder than I thought it would be. Sometimes I feel like the Lone Ranger."

He laughed. "I know what you mean. Just let me know, okay?"

She nodded and quickly left.

The rest of the day went by quickly. The weekend crew got the pizza, which made Bradley and Charlie happy. Anya found out the supplier had mislabeled the components that were shipped to All Pro. Anya and her buyers had an urgent call with the supplier to say that that was unacceptable. The supplier agreed to expedite a shipment of the right components to be delivered by noon on Tuesday.

By the end of the day, Jeremy felt better about his work with his team. He was already using what he had learned from Josephine. But it seemed like he'd spent most of the day dealing with issues related to the Symmetry shipment.

The Up and Down Week

He walked into work on Wednesday still feeling good about his work with his employees. That good attitude evaporated shortly after he walked by the production line on his way to his office. This morning, instead of the usual hum of equipment and people, there was the sound of equipment being taken apart. Something was wrong. Jeremy saw Charlie and Bradley by Bradley's desk. Bradley was quietly standing with his arms crossed while Charlie was waving and talking at Bradley, not to him.

Charlie saw Jeremy approaching and gave a heads up to Bradley. They both turned toward Jeremy. Jeremy said, "This doesn't look good. What's going on?"

Bradley said in an exasperated tone, "The equipment at the inspection station has broken down, and it's being fixed now."

Almost before Bradley could finish, Charlie jumped in. "The production staff doesn't know how to use the equipment, and that's why it broke down."

Bradley shook his head in frustration. "Don't blame my team." Then he looked at Jeremy. "That equipment wasn't designed for such a high volume, and that's why it broke down." He glanced first at Charlie and then at Jeremy. "My team was using it correctly."

Jeremy felt his anxiety level go up. He didn't pause and take a deep breath. Abruptly, he said, "My bottom line is getting good parts shipped to Symmetry by Friday. Are you going to be able to get the line back up so we can meet our commitment?" He looked at both Bradley and Charlie.

Bradley said, "I'm 90 percent sure we'll be able to. The repair team is making good progress. If we can get the equipment fixed this afternoon, we'll be able to make up the lost time on the defective parts. But it'll delay shipments to other customers."

"Good. Well, not good on the other customers, but I'm glad to hear we'll be able to get that shipment out." He was relieved.

Charlie had been holding back. "Who's paying for the repairs? If I have to pay, I'll be over budget in Q1."

"The inspection equipment, including repairs, is your team's expense," said Bradley.

Seeing the argument would disintegrate into a no-win situation, Jeremy jumped in, saying, "It doesn't matter who pays for it. All that matters is getting the line up and running again."

Immediately, he got questioning looks from both of them. "You both look surprised."

Charlie said, "You said it doesn't matter who pays for it. It always has in the past. If I have to pay, I'll be over budget this quarter. Last year, Ted wrote me up for that."

Looking first at Charlie and then at Bradley, Jeremy asked, "Did you budget for repairs this year?"

Charlie quickly replied, "Yes, but then my budget was cut in half when we were setting budgets in December, before you started." Bradley just looked down.

Jeremy said, "Well, just book it to the usual location. We need to know how much we're spending on repairs. But I guarantee you won't be written up for getting the line up and running."

Relief flooded Charlie's face. "Good. You don't know what that was like."

"Okay then. Do you need anything from me to get everything moving?" He smiled. "More pizza?"

Both Charlie and Bradley laughed. Bradley said, "No, we're good. Too much pizza will spoil us."

There were more ups and downs that week. They had to treat the inspection equipment with kid gloves to keep it working, and it was slowing repairs down.

Sean struggled to get his plans done on time. Jeremy found himself sitting down with him to go through his plans in detail. The rework on Symmetry's parts, in addition to the line being down, had thrown their production schedules into chaos.

Stress levels were running high. Everyone knew the risk of not getting the parts to Symmetry by Friday.

Thanks to all the scrambling, all the repaired parts left All Pro for Symmetry on Thursday at 5:00 p.m. They would be there by 7:00 a.m. Friday, meeting Symmetry's deadline.

Jeremy was tired, and he could tell everyone on his staff was too. He made a point to walk around and thank every staff member in person.

Jeremy went back to his desk and sent a summary email to Ken and his own staff regarding the status of the shipment. In the email, he thanked his staff members for their contributions in turning around the shipment so quickly. Then, he scheduled a staff meeting at 1:00 p.m. Friday afternoon so he could share his goals for the team and his personal strengths and weaknesses.

Sharing His Goals, Strengths, and Weaknesses

Jeremy spent much of Friday morning going through the mountain of emails that had built up during the week. He felt reasonably caught up when he walked into the conference room shortly before the 1:00 p.m. staff meeting. Bradley was already there, as usual.

"Jeremy, I need to talk to you." He pulled a few sheets of paper from a file folder and handed them to Jeremy.

"They're emails from Sean. He sent the first one to Symmetry, giving them an earlier delivery date than the one we agreed on for their next shipment. I told everyone when production would be done, and Charlie tacked on his time for quality control. Everyone knew our date."

Jeremy was aghast. "You're kidding. We can't do that. I'll have to call them."

"I already called their production manager. I told her the date in the email was an error and gave her the real one. Thankfully, she accepted it."

Jeremy scoured the emails, a sour feeling in his stomach. Although Sean was in charge of planning, he wasn't supposed to change schedule commitments to customers without Jeremy's approval.

"Thanks for calling them right away. I could see them blowing up again." Jeremy felt sick thinking about what could have happened if Bradley hadn't intervened.

He started the 1:00 p.m. staff meeting by thanking the team for getting the replacement shipment turned around so quickly. Pausing briefly, he said he knew Friday afternoon meetings were unusual, but he had something personal to share that he thought was important. Immediately, looks of concern popped up around the table.

"You're not leaving, are you?" Anya asked.

Jeremy realized he'd set them up for bad news. "No, I'm not. I want to acknowledge it's been a little crazy for us since I started in this job." He saw several nods when he said that. "I want to take time today to share my goals for this team and how we work together."

The looks of concern were replaced by curiosity. He continued, "I know manufacturing has had a rough couple of years. And we have some very aggressive goals to meet this year. To hit those goals, we need to perform at our peak, as a team. I believe we have to be a high-performance team where there's trust, great communication, teamwork, commitment, and success. I want each of you to feel like you can do your best work here and be successful."

Looking around, he saw a mix of reactions. Anya was nodding her head in agreement. Others looked neutral or even wary.

Continuing, he said, "A high-performance team starts with a strong foundation of trust. Beginning with me. You need to trust me, and I need to trust you. But I think it'll be easier to trust me if you know more about me and what makes me tick."

He opened up his notebook. "To speed that up, I want to share some insights about me, especially my strengths and weaknesses." If he was reading the group right, most seemed surprised and curious.

He quickly added, "It won't take long, and I bet you already know some of this." He walked through his strengths and also his weaknesses when he overused his strengths. He ended by saying, "I tend to focus on tasks, being efficient, and getting things done. That's where my mind goes. I don't tend to focus on the people side of things so much. So, if I seem short and focused on next steps, please remember that's how I'm wired. It's not intentional. I know it can create issues for some of you, and I need to learn when to curb my tendencies. My request is for you to remind me when I'm missing something or not giving you what you need or want from me."

He looked at Anya, and she held his eyes. Then he said, "I do have one request. I value being efficient. It will help if you are prepared and organized when we meet. Even for topics with the whole team. Look at the agenda ahead of time and be prepared if a topic applies to you. And my second request is to give me early warning if you see a potential issue on the horizon. I don't like surprises. I know that's probably not a surprise for some of you."

There was silence, and then Anya laughed. "That explains a lot. Thanks for telling us about yourself." Her eyes slid from Jeremy, to Bradley, and back. "You two have a lot in common."

Bradley replied, "You might be right. I like being efficient, and I don't like surprises. I can identify with a lot of what you said. That's kind of scary."

Gia started talking then, and the team got into a discussion about their similarities and differences. Jeremy concluded the discussion by asking, "Would you be interested in doing the same exercise with the team?" Everyone but Charlie and Bradley said yes. He made a mental note to follow up with both.

Jeremy also told them he'd schedule regular one-on-one meetings with each of them to find out more about them. Everyone seemed satisfied with that. Jeremy ended the meeting, asking Sean to stay behind.

Jeremy was blunt with Sean. "Bradley showed me your emails to Symmetry. What is this date here?" He put the emails on the table in front of Sean.

"They were bugging me a lot. They won't leave me alone. So, I gave them an earlier date." He sat up straighter when he noticed the look on Jeremy's face.

"Sean," Jeremy began, rubbing his temples, "why didn't you let me know? All you had to do was tell me, and I could've handled it. That's my job. If Bradley hadn't caught it, we could've lost their contract. The next time a customer emails you, send it my way."

Sean mumbled something and shot out the door.

Jeremy had to do something about Sean. He was becoming a liability. He was taking too much time and effort to clean up after, especially with all the other issues Jeremy had on his plate.

Ken Drops "The Bomb"

On Monday morning, Jeremy stopped by the production area to check with Bradley on getting the production line back to normal after the previous week's chaos.

Jeremy said, "I bet you're looking forward to having a normal week."

"Yes, but we have a lot of catching up to do," Bradley replied.

"I was looking at this week's shipment plan last night, and I see that. Let me know if you run into any issues. At least we won't have Symmetry breathing down our necks."

Bradley grudgingly said, "Yep. It's good to get that out of the way."

"I'll let you get back to your team, but thanks again for getting the shipment out Thursday. You and your team went above and beyond."

Bradley paused for a moment, and then his face broke into a smile and he said, "Thanks, Jeremy. I appreciate that."

Jeremy went to his desk feeling good about his discussion with Bradley. He thought, I see what Josephine means about taking the time to connect one on one and focusing on the positive.

But Jeremy's positive vibe was short lived. Ken walked into his office a little after ten that morning. It was a bad sign whenever Ken came to his office. He closed Jeremy's office door and sat down. "We have huge issues with Symmetry."

Caught off guard, Jeremy stammered, "We got them their shipment on time, and all the parts were 100 percent good. Did something happen?"

"Their CEO called Richard last night. Apparently, their production team had to work all weekend to install our 'good' parts in their assemblies to meet their customer's deadline. They had cost overruns, and they're bent out of shape. They're blaming us. Their CEO gave Richard an ultimatum." Then he hesitated, looking out Jeremy's window.

Jeremy leaned forward. "Which was?"

Ken looked back now at Jeremy. "He told Richard we need to improve both quality and on-time delivery." He paused. "Or they'll go to another supplier."

"How much improvement do they want?"

"They want our quality level at 99 percent and 98 percent on-time delivery. By the end of the year. I know that's a big improvement."

"By the end of the year? That's less than eleven months from now. That'd be an eight-point improvement for on-time delivery over our Q1 goals. And quality. That'd be a four-point increase. We're not going to hit our Q1 goals. I don't know how we'll do it." His mind was spinning.

"You delivered Symmetry's replacement shipment. You can build off that."

Now, Ken was almost sounding like a cheerleader. Jeremy would have found that amusing if the situation hadn't been so dire.

"Ken, we'd have to make so many changes in so many areas. We're having issues with our own suppliers. The production line isn't in very good shape. I've got issues with planning." He hesitated, not sure he wanted to admit it to Ken, but he blurted out, "And my team isn't working well together."

Ken said, "I know you haven't been in your job very long, but we can't afford to lose Symmetry. If you need to make changes on your team, make them. If you need to fix the line, tell me how much. I'll take it to Richard." He shook his head and looked out the window again. "If we lose Symmetry, I think we'll both be out of a job."

Ken's admission surprised Jeremy. Ken wasn't the type to share personal concerns. Dumbfounded, Jeremy sat back, still processing Symmetry's demands.

Ken stood up. He was done with their conversation. "Let me know what you need from me." Not waiting for a reply from Jeremy, he started to walk out the door.

"Does anyone else know about this ultimatum? I need to tell my team, but I need to figure out what to say. And how to say it. Any guidance?"

"I have confidence in you, Jeremy. You just need to tackle this like you would one of your engineering dilemmas. Just don't wait too long."

Ken's comments increased Jeremy's anxiety. He felt overwhelmed. For a moment, the thought crossed his mind that he should start looking for another job. Then he felt guilty. He'd be leaving his team and Ken in a lurch. Then he thought of Josephine.

He called Roast and, thankfully, she was there. She agreed to meet him for a quick lunch at El Ranchito, a taco shop down the street from Roast.

Once they were seated with their burritos, Jeremy told Josephine about his conversation with Ken. He concluded by saying, "I don't know how we can do it. And if we lose Symmetry's business, I'm done."

Josephine had been listening intently. "Have you told your staff yet?"

"Not yet. We barely got that shipment back to Symmetry. It didn't go smoothly, and now we have this. I'm trying to figure out how to sell them on the idea that we can hit these goals."

She was silent for a minute. "You know you can't sell them on this. You shouldn't even try."

He shrugged his shoulders. "If I don't, I'm afraid they'll give up. Or quit."

"Did you try what we discussed the last time we met?"

Feeling impatient, he replied, "I did. Yes." He wanted to jump into his new, huge problem.

She followed up with, "And how did that go?"

He forced himself to think about the last week. "I focused on just connecting with my staff. And I talked to the team about my goals for the team and my strengths. It seemed to go well. But that's not going to fix my new super-problem."

"Good. I know it's only been a few days. But did it seem to make a difference?"

She wasn't going to drop it. He thought back to his interactions last week. "Yes, I think it did. People seemed . . ." He paused, trying to find the right word. "Appreciative. They seemed to warm up a little bit."

"Good. You started building trust with your team. You should keep up the good work," she said with an encouraging voice. "But that will all be lost if you try to sell them on hitting those goals. You'll go back to zero on the trust meter. Maybe negative. They won't believe you if you don't believe it. That's why I suggest not 'selling' them."

He was feeling like he was at the end of his rope. "Any recommendations on what I should tell them?"

"First, be honest with them. Tell them what you know. And tell them what you don't know. That'll probably include that you don't know how to hit those numbers. But tell them you need their help to make it happen."

"Okay. I understand the honesty. But I feel like I need to give them a direction. Some hope." Looking at her intently, he said, "I need strategies. I don't have time to go through the mechanics of engaging employees or building a vision. We don't need a vision. We need to hit Symmetry's demands. What can I do to deliver breakthrough strategies?" He felt like he was begging, but he was willing to beg.

"You won't be set up for success if you don't do the steps before jumping into strategy. Right now, you have big issues with finger-pointing and some of your staff not doing their jobs, and they're not working well together. If you jump directly to strategies right now, you're working on quicksand. You need to build a foundation." She was emphatic. "Adding these 'impossible' demands, as you call them, is going to throw fuel on the fire."

He thought about his team and what he was seeing. "You might be right." He opened his notebook to the five steps and stared at each of them. They made complete sense, but his sense of urgency was taking over his cramped mind. He remembered what Sasha said and took a deep breath. "If you were in my shoes, what would you tell my staff?"

"I'd tell them your goals for the team haven't changed. That you want to have the team become a high-performance team where there's great teamwork and success. Only a high-performance team will have a shot at delivering Symmetry's demands. That'll be your focus over the next several months."

"I'm not sure even the highest-performing team could hit those goals. Or if the team will be patient enough to do the other steps before getting to solutions." He paused, thinking about his own mental state. "Kind of like me."

She smiled. Then she asked, "What are your chances of hitting those demands with your team functioning the way it is right now?"

Begrudgingly, he had to admit she had him. "Like, zero."

She said, "If your employees see their relationship with you growing and the team improving, that'll keep them committed to your cause. Even in bleak situations, people will go above and beyond for the people they work with, if they feel really good about the team and the people. You're going to need that."

"You're right. I am." He thought about his next steps. "I'll tell the team about Symmetry this afternoon. I don't want them hearing through the grapevine."

"Good. I hope that goes well." She pulled out her iPhone. "I see we're meeting tomorrow morning, right?"

He nodded and said, "Yes."

She grabbed her trash and, standing up, said, "I've got to go. We'll talk about step 2 tomorrow."

He nodded, saying, "Yes, on to step 2."

With that, they both went back to work.

Being Honest with the Team

When he returned to work, Jeremy sent an urgent voicemail to his staff telling them there'd be a mandatory staff meeting at 2:00 p.m.

When everyone was seated, he got right to the point. "Thanks for breaking away so quickly to be here. I wanted to let you know before you heard it through the rumor mill. Our goals for the rest of the year just got a lot harder." Then Jeremy told them about the discussion he'd had with Ken in the morning.

Shock registered on everybody's face except for Sean's. Sean didn't seem to get the implications.

Charlie was the first to speak. "What? We're supposed to magically improve quality to 99 percent by the end of the year. We're not going to hit our Q1 goal of 95 percent by a long shot. It's already the middle of February. How are we supposed to do that?"

Bradley was next. "And we have to get to 98 percent on-time delivery when we're at 80 percent so far in Q1. We won't get anywhere close to our Q1 goal of 90 percent. Symmetry gives us hardly any notice on their order changes. Are they going to change the way they manage their orders? I bet not." He pushed back in his seat, arms crossed.

Always looking at the bottom line, Gia asked, "If we don't deliver, will they go to another supplier?"

"They told Richard they have another company that can deliver those improvements next year. At least we have the opportunity to be the first to deliver what they want," Jeremy said, trying to be more positive than he felt.

Bradley was shaking his head. "I wonder if that's Smith Manufacturing, the new company that opened last year in Oakland. They've been pushing their specs, although I've heard mixed things about their ability to deliver on their promises."

"It doesn't really sound like it matters at this point," Anya said.

Sean had just been watching the discussion. He asked, "Would it really be impossible to hit those goals?"

Bradley looked at him in disbelief. "Have you been watching our numbers? We're so far off in Q1, and now our goals have been ramped up. A lot. It will take a lot of investment, and the sun, the moon, and all the planets will have to align to get there."

Jeremy jumped in before the discussion got more negative. "I have to admit, I don't have a solution right now. These goals are very aggressive. I don't want anyone to think they're not. But we have a lot of capability in this group to come up with a plan. I do know that, if we can start operating as a high-performance team, our chances of success go way up. So that's what I'm going to be focusing on. I'll be following through to schedule the one-on-one meetings we discussed last Friday. And I'm extending our Tuesday staff meetings to two hours starting tomorrow. We need to put a plan in place."

Bradley wasn't making eye contact with him. He looked like he was elsewhere. Jeremy made a mental note to talk to him after the meeting. "We'll talk about next steps at staff tomorrow."

With that, everyone stood up to walk out. Jeremy asked Bradley to stay behind for a minute. Following Josephine's advice, he was going to lean into a discussion with Bradley about his reaction to the news.

Jeremy said, "After I shared the news, you looked really down. I wanted to check in with you to see how you're doing." And then he waited.

Bradley looked at him and then turned away. Finally, he said, "I just don't know if I'm up for this. Especially after last week. Last week was really hard. And these goals. Wow." He stopped for a moment. "It's going to be a long year, with this group and these goals. Don't get me wrong. It's not you. I see you're trying to make a difference. But it's not working for me right now."

"What do you mean by 'it's not working'?"

"I'm responsible for production, and I don't know how we'll ever be able to hit those numbers. I'm downstream of everyone else's work. I have to rely on good parts from procurement, good plans from Sean, good quality systems from Charlie, and so on. So, all their mistakes and problems wind up affecting me and my team. And the end result is my team and I have to put in a lot of long, late hours."

Jeremy said, "It's not just you. Charlie's quality team worked a lot of hours too. And I know there were mistakes, but everyone's doing the best they can."

"That's part of the problem," Bradley said. Turning toward Jeremy, he continued. "I'm not sure everyone even knows what they're responsible for. Or that everyone can really do their job."

Jeremy paused and realized how tired Bradley looked. "Last week was frustrating and tiring. For everyone. I know the mistakes really affected you and your team. I appreciate what you did that allowed us to get that shipment out. And I know it's not sustainable."

As he was saying that, a lightbulb went on in his head. He realized how right Josephine had been. "Bradley, we haven't had a strong team foundation. I see that now with being the manager over the last six weeks. We can build that together. But I can't do it by myself. I need you and what you bring to manufacturing. We'll build a strong team and go after Symmetry's goals. It'll be challenging, but we'll be a stronger team, and I think work will be more enjoyable."

"Work enjoyable?" Bradley asked. "I'd like to see that."

Jeremy wanted to keep the discussion going. He had a crazy idea.

"Tell you what. Do you like to make bets?"

"Like, what? Work becomes enjoyable?" Bradley said sarcastically.

"Yes, on December 31, you'll say you like coming to work," Jeremy said.

"Ha. That's not even a work day," Bradley said.

Chuckling, Jeremy replied, "You get my point."

Bradley was quiet. It looked like he was considering Jeremy's offer. "And what's the wager?"

Jeremy studied Bradley's face, trying to figure out what he was thinking. Then he saw his hair. It looked like Bradley's hairline was beginning to recede. "The loser has to shave his head."

"What? Really?" Bradley said, looking at him as if he couldn't believe what Jeremy had offered. Then he smiled. "I'll take your bet. This is going to be easy. By the way, I used to shave my head. Have you?"

"No. Once I almost had to. In college." Jeremy remembered his fraternity brothers who did. The end result hadn't been good for any of them.

Bradley's smile disappeared then. He said, "I still reserve the right to quit between now and the end of the year. Then, all bets are off."

Jeremy nodded his head. "Of course. That goes without saying for everyone on the team. Staying with the company is a choice."

Bradley picked up his laptop and walked out, leaving Jeremy to think about what he'd do if Bradley quit. He didn't have any good answers.

STEP 2

Engage the Employees

Tuesday, February 14

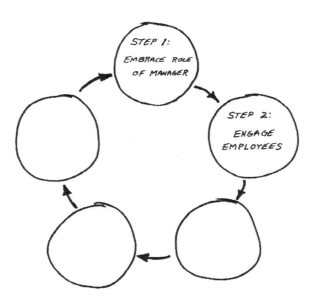

Josephine's Advice on Engagement

Jeremy and Josephine were scheduled to meet at 7:00 a.m. Tuesday morning. She was delayed a bit, so Jeremy had time to jot down some notes. Top of mind for him was figuring out what to do with his staff.

He was still thinking about his discussion with Bradley when Josephine joined him.

"You look worried," she said.

"I am worried." Then he told her about his staff meeting and the discussion with Bradley afterward.

Shaking her head, she said, "Well, now I understand your concern. It sounds like Bradley would be a big loss. Do you have any replacements in mind?"

He grimaced. "No, I don't. And I have issues with other employees too."

"We talked about Sean before. Who else?"

"Anya, for one. We're having ongoing issues with suppliers, and her team's struggling. She's struggling."

"What about Gia and Charlie?" she asked.

"Charlie's pretty good at the day-to-day quality management, but I'm going to need somebody who can come up with a strategic plan. Especially with the goals we have from Symmetry." He shifted in his seat. "Gia's fine in her role. She totally handles logistics, and she seems to have a good team. But she doesn't go out of her way to help other areas out. Like production. And Bradley is so competent in his job. That's why losing him would create such a big hole."

A puzzled look appeared on her face. "Have you talked to each of your employees about their roles and your concerns?"

"Not yet. I've been in firefighting mode. I'm going to set up one-on-one meetings."

"It's good you've thought about your employees and their fit in their jobs. Getting the right people on the team is critical to your success and a good place to start step 2."

"That's good to know."

"Hold on," she said. "First things first. Before you decide whether someone is a fit for their job, you should make sure you get clarity with them on their responsibilities and deliverables."

"I've been very direct with Sean on his." Then he thought about the others. "I haven't talked to Anya or Charlie about responsibilities. I've just been talking to them about what they need to do to get shipments out."

"Okay. Let's talk about the next part of step 2, which is to get that role clarity. It's important for everyone on the team to know who's responsible for what and what they're expected to deliver."

"I think everyone knows what their job is and everyone else's too." He wasn't sure where she was going with this.

"In my experience, everyone thinks it's obvious who does what. But I find that's often not the case, especially for the gray areas."

"Gray areas? Do you mean where it's not clear who does what?"

"Exactly. Usually it's because different people own different parts of the process," she explained. "That's often behind the blaming and finger pointing you've talked about."

He thought about last week and said, "I think supplier quality has some gray areas, especially between Charlie, Anya, and Bradley. I'm not sure who does what on supplier quality myself. It seems to change depending on the situation. I've had to intervene several times."

"Yes," she said, nodding in agreement. "That's when the ball gets dropped and you have to figure out what happened. Everyone gets frustrated."

"So how would you suggest we get that clarity?"

"Have them write their own position profiles. And make sure they go after those gray areas."

She made it sound so easy. "I know they're going to push back on writing them. They're going to say they know everyone's role and they're too busy."

"That's why your approach is important. You want each of your employees to 'own' their role on the team. Right?"

"Definitely."

"So, everyone should document their own role. Who knows their position better? You or them?"

"They do, of course."

"Exactly. So, everyone writes their own. Including you. You do yours first."

"So, if I write mine, then they'll be compelled to write theirs. Is that what you're thinking?"

"That's what I do with my employees. They can't argue when I do mine first." She continued, "When your employees write their own position profiles, give them the responsibility of working through the gray areas. It sounds like it's time to get those gray areas on the table. It'll give them a sense of ownership, and they'll have to work together to figure it out. You're killing two birds with one stone, so to speak."

Jotting notes down, Jeremy said, "Yeah, if they don't kill each other in the process. Do you have a position profile you'd recommend?"

"You can come up with the format. My only recommendation is to keep it simple. Make sure everyone documents their major responsibilities and the expectations for each responsibility."

"Expectation for each responsibility? Do you mean the outcome they should achieve? The result?"

"Exactly. The result should be specific and what a strong performer would deliver. For example, one of my responsibilities is to identify and contract with coffee farms to consistently supply high-quality, organic coffee beans. They must meet Roast's cost goals and demonstrate to me that they're a trustworthy supplier, meaning that when I order it, they ship it so it's delivered in the time frame I specify. Make sense?"

"Yes," he said with a sigh as he wrote down her example. "That really hits home because we haven't been able to meet those criteria for our own customers. Our parts are very hard to make, but we should be doing better."

Reading back her example to her, he said, "Anya has that same responsibility for our company. She doesn't buy beans, but she manages all purchasing."

Nodding her head, Josephine said, "Yes, she should have it, and you could specify the level of quality her suppliers need to meet. That's what you're going to need to deliver those Symmetry goals. Right?"

"Yep. It should be understood that that's her responsibility. We need to document it and then discuss it," he replied.

"Exactly. You should discuss the position profile for each of your employees in your one-on-one meetings. Your goal in that discussion is to make sure you align on responsibilities and expectations. And, most importantly, you should discuss how you can support their success in the role."

He added notes to his notebook. "Some will need more support from me than others. Anya and Charlie will need more support. Gia and Bradley will need less."

"Right. You should have a discussion with each of them and get agreement. Like Charlie may need your direction to develop a strategic plan for quality. Anya may need your help on some aspects of supplier management. In other areas, they may just need some coaching. You still need to meet with all of them. Even Gia and Bradley may need your support if they run into bumps on the road. They should all walk away knowing you want to help them be successful. That'll also build more trust with each employee."

He added to his notes and looked at his list of employees. He'd left the tough one for last. "What about Sean? Despite all the direction I've given him and others have provided, he's not listening. Or, if he is, he's just not changing his approach. I don't know what else I can do."

She looked at him for a moment. "I've inherited situations like that. He's been in the job nine months?"

"Yes, he has. I know it's not long, but he's not improving. By now, he should be up to speed in the job. And he's not listening and learning."

"It sounds like you've decided you need to replace him," she said.

"Yes, I have. And others are really frustrated by him too." He was thinking specifically of Bradley and Gia.

"You can't have someone who isn't doing a good job and is negatively affecting the team. If you don't deal with his performance, you'll undermine your team's confidence in you as the leader."

Jeremy sat back. "Do I just fire him? I've never fired anybody before." He felt like a deer in the headlights.

She smiled and shook her head no. "I still think you should go through this exercise with him too. If you've really given him feedback and he's not changing his behavior, it shouldn't be the same discussion.

You need to remind him you've given him a lot of feedback and his performance has to immediately improve or he faces being terminated. He needs to know where he stands. That'll set the stage for terminating him if it comes to that. You should talk to your HR team though."

"Okay. I'm not looking forward to that whole thing."

"Don't worry. You won't be alone. Your HR team will help," Josephine said. "Just don't let Sean get in the way of coaching and supporting your good employees."

He got her point.

He looked at his notes. He'd been lukewarm when Josephine had proposed the idea of the position profiles, but he was beginning to like the idea more and more. "So, after I have those individual discussions, I'll have everyone share their position profile with the rest of the team. Right? That way, there shouldn't be any confusion on who's responsible for what. That'll help."

"Yes, it will," she said, glancing at her watch. "Whoops. I need to go. Any other burning questions or issues?"

"No. I've got what I need. Thanks, Josephine. This has been great. As usual."

He was ready for step 2 with his team, he thought to himself as he drove to work. At his weekly staff meeting that afternoon, he'd tell the team about writing their position profiles. And by next Tuesday, he'd have his profile ready to review with them.

Tripping over Each Other

After his meeting with Josephine, Jeremy walked into work with high expectations for the rest of the week. He was almost at his desk when he received a text message from Charlie asking him to come to the production floor. Charlie had included the word "urgent" in his message. *Oh crap*, Jeremy thought, hurrying down to production.

He found Anya, Bradley, and Charlie off to the side of the production area. They were having a heated argument when he arrived. He heard Bradley talking to Anya in a very loud voice, and Charlie was watching with his arms crossed. Everyone was clearly unhappy. They didn't see him coming. He got close enough to hear Bradley tell Anya, "You have to get your supplier to replace those parts by tomorrow morning. Or else."

Bradley had crossed the line, and Jeremy knew he'd need to address it. But now, he needed to understand the situation.

Anya was clearly angry. "Or else what?" It was a demand. Not a question.

Bradley was just beginning to reply when Jeremy arrived. "Good morning. This doesn't sound good. What's going on?"

There was an awkward silence before Bradley said, "We have another quality issue with a part we're short on. We may miss our next Symmetry shipment."

Jeremy felt his anxiety level go up. He said, "We can't afford that. Can we work around it? Sort for good parts? Fix parts?" He was trying to offer as many options as possible.

Bradley replied, "We're starting to sort through parts on hand, but we're short. The production plan had an error in the delivery date we didn't catch, and we're short two hundred parts." Jeremy made a note to follow up with Sean on the delivery date error.

Charlie chimed in. "About twenty percent of the parts are bad. At that rate, we'll be forty short for this week's build."

Anya said in a defensive voice, "I called the sales manager at the supplier two weeks ago and told them their parts had too many defects. I thought they'd fixed their process control system."

Bradley replied, "That's not enough. Didn't you follow up with them?"

"I asked you to do an inspection when the parts first arrived. Didn't one of you do that?" She looked at both Bradley and Charlie.

Charlie said, "That's not my job and . . ."

Before he could say any more, Jeremy jumped in. "That isn't going to get us anywhere right now. It sounds like we need to get good parts in." He turned to Anya and asked her to call the supplier immediately.

Anya, glaring at Bradley, said, "I'll call them as soon as I get to my desk. I'll expedite a shipment of good parts to be here tomorrow. I know that's the best they can do."

"Okay, good," Jeremy replied. "Can you let all of us know as soon as they've confirmed?" Then, remembering his tendency to ignore people's emotional needs, he said, "And I know you'll get to the bottom of this. Let me know though if I can help."

"Thanks, Jeremy. I appreciate your support, and I will," Anya said, glancing at Bradley.

Looking at all three, Jeremy said, "Let me know how I can help. We have to get this next shipment to Symmetry on time, and the quality needs to be 100 percent." They all nodded in agreement. Looking at his watch, he said, "I have to get to my next meeting, but you know where to find me." They went their respective ways. No one was happy.

The hallway meeting reinforced the need to get roles on the team figured out, especially around supplier quality. And he needed to deal with Sean's performance. And maybe Anya's too. And Bradley's comment. Suddenly he felt tired, and it was still early in the day.

The staff meeting that afternoon was tense as they planned how to get the Symmetry shipment out on time. Anya reported that her supplier would be delivering replacement parts that were 100 percent inspected by the end of the day on Tuesday.

As a group, they walked through the production plan to determine how to free time up on the production line to make the Symmetry shipment. Bradley, Charlie, and Gia's teams would all need to work overtime on Wednesday and Thursday to make the shipment. Jeremy asked Bradley and Gia to send him their estimates of the additional labor costs. Everyone was clearly frustrated. The unexpected discussion of the week's shipments took up almost the entire time even though Jeremy had extended it from one to two hours. Jeremy didn't talk to them about writing their position profiles.

He and his team struggled the entire week. He and Sean went through Sean's spreadsheet to find the source of his error. He met with Anya and her buyers to understand what had been communicated to the supplier of the defective part. After that meeting, Jeremy had a better appreciation for Anya's challenges when he found out how new her buyers were to their roles.

Remembering Josephine's advice, Jeremy met with Bradley to discuss his "or else" comment to Anya. Before he met with Bradley, he planned the key points he wanted to cover. He needed to confirm what had happened and give Bradley the chance to respond. Then, he'd need to remind Bradley of the impact on Anya and the team and ask him to modify his communications. Finally, he needed to close by telling Bradley how much he valued having him on the team.

When Bradley walked in, Jeremy started the conversation. "When I walked up to you, Anya, and Charlie, I heard you tell Anya that she'd better replace those parts by a certain time, or else. It came across to me, and I think to Anya too, as very negative, almost like a threat. So, I wanted to get your perspective."

Surprise registered on Bradley's face. "Really? As a threat? That wasn't my intention. I was trying to say 'or else we're going to miss our shipment.'" He paused and then shook his head. "I guess you could have heard it as a threat. I do remember Anya reacting strongly. I don't remember exactly what she said." He looked at Jeremy.

"I think she said, 'Or what?' So, yes, I'm 99 percent sure she heard it as a threat."

Bradley sat back with a look of regret. "I need to apologize to her. That's not what I meant at all."

"An apology would be good."

"Are we done? I want to talk to Anya right now." Bradley stood up.

"Bradley, I just need to ask that you think about what you say to others on the team. I think we both are so focused on results that sometimes we miss how we affect others. I know I do. We need good relationships and teamwork. Okay?"

"Okay. I see that, and I'll try to remember it. Let me talk to Anya." He stood up to walk out.

Jeremy said, "Bradley, you bring so much to the team. You can help the team be stronger too."

"Thanks," Bradley said, heading out the door.

Jeremy was glad to see that Bradley wanted to talk to Anya immediately.

They did get the Symmetry shipment out on time on Friday, but it required more late nights for everyone.

Over the weekend, Jeremy worked on his own position profile. He started by using the job description Ken had given him when he had first applied for the manufacturing manager job. It included an overall two-sentence purpose of his position. He'd then listed eight core responsibilities and specific expectations for each responsibility. He'd review it later Monday morning with Ken and then share it with his staff at their regular Tuesday staff meeting.

Getting Past Firefighting and Starting Position Profiles

Jeremy started the staff meeting by reminding his staff that their meetings would now be two hours long. He said, "We seem to spend all our time in staff scrambling to just get shipments out on time during the week. We never have time to discuss anything else. So, a longer staff meeting will give us more time to get ahead. I want to keep reviewing shipments for the week, but we need to start looking at shipments that are going out two, three, or four weeks from now. Make sense?"

"It would really help," Bradley said. Others nodded around the table.

"Good," Jeremy said. "We need to understand which shipments are at risk before they become a problem."

Gia said, "That's a great idea. To get ahead in the game."

"I'm glad you said that, Gia. I was going to talk to you after staff, but I'm hoping you could lead that effort for us. You'll need to work with Sean to see what shipments are planned and then work with each of the staff to make sure we're prepared with parts and so forth."

For a moment, her face registered surprise.

He quickly said, "I see you weren't expecting that. You don't have to agree to it right now. Let's talk more, and then you can decide. I know it's above and beyond your current role. Okay?"

"That would be good," she answered, her face transformed back to her usual confident look.

"Excellent. Let's review shipments for this week."

For once, all shipments were expected to go out on time and no quality issues were expected. Jeremy told the team, "This is great to see. I think this is the first week since I've been manufacturing manager we aren't going to have to scramble. Thank you, and tell your teams thank you too."

Everybody nodded their heads in agreement. Gia asked, "Was there something different about this week? For things to go so smoothly?"

Everyone looked around. "We didn't have any late changes to orders," Bradley said.

Anya added, "I don't think we had any issues with our suppliers pop up either."

"That is great news. Let's hope that continues."

The team was in an upbeat mood for once. Jeremy knew that would change with the next agenda item.

He said, "Now, we're changing topics. We had another challenging week last week just to get shipments out on time. And it's not the first time. When I step back, I consistently see issues around role clarity. Like who's responsible for what."

He got questioning looks from everyone around the table. Gia said, "It sounds like you think we don't know our jobs and who does what."

She wasn't the only one with that concern based on everyone else's faces. Jeremy replied, "I think you know what your own job is. But I'm not sure everyone else does, including me. We need to get agreement on everyone's responsibilities and expected results."

Anya said, "I don't know if I'm the only one who's confused, but you lost me there."

Jeremy realized others were confused too. "No, you're not the only one. Sorry. I didn't explain myself very well." He looked around.

"We have very challenging goals as a team from Symmetry this year. Right?"

Everyone nodded in agreement.

"We are the team responsible for hitting those goals. Our individual responsibilities have to reflect what we'll each need to deliver so that our team is successful. Does that help?"

As he looked around, he wasn't sure he'd been clear enough. "Each of us is going to write our own position profile," he said, passing around a stack of papers. "What I'm giving you is the position profile I wrote for my own job. You can see what I'm looking for. It's just two pages long. Feel free to ask questions."

The team was quiet as he read his profile, including the purpose of the role, the major responsibilities, and the expectations. "I was specific with my results. For example, I wrote that I'm responsible for ensuring I have capable manufacturing staff members who are successful in their jobs. The result of that responsibility will be that each staff member will successfully deliver his or her goals."

He paused then to look around. He could see they were thinking about that responsibility because he was talking about them. He said, "I think each of you has a similar responsibility. You have employees too, and, if they're successful, you'll be successful." He glanced at Sean for a moment. "Except for Sean, of course. He doesn't have any employees reporting to him."

He could see everyone thinking about it. Anya broke the silence. "It makes sense. So, you expect us to include that. But what if we determine we can't meet that expectation? If we think we don't have capable employees?" Her voice was strained.

He could see everyone looking at him. He wondered how many had concerns about their employees. "Do you mean you don't have a staff that can deliver the results you need? If that's the case, we need to figure that out really quickly. Especially with the Symmetry challenge."

"Okay," she said. Her voice didn't sound okay. Jeremy made a mental note to talk to her after the meeting.

Pausing briefly to see if anyone else had questions or concerns,

Jeremy asked, "Are you ready to move on?" No one said anything. He continued, "I'm not sure how to read your silence, but we'll push ahead. That may answer some questions. I also want to make sure we address those gray areas that get us in trouble."

"What do you mean, 'gray areas'?" Gia asked with a frown.

He explained, "It's those areas where it's not clear who has responsibility for a task, and it's usually when people have different parts of a process. Like last week's discussion about incoming parts and quality. We all need to know who does what."

He could see frustration on Charlie, Bradley, and Anya's faces, but no one said anything.

"To get more clarity, I want you to document your role, including responsibilities and expected results." He was greeted by stony silence. "This will bring clarity to all of us. We're going to take the next ten minutes in this meeting so you can start your position profile."

He handed everyone a rough outline for a position profile and set a timer on his phone.

They were still working on them when Jeremy said, "I know you're not done, but let's see what you've got. Who wants to be first?"

"I'll start," Gia offered. Jeremy gave her an encouraging smile as she held up her paper. "As the logistics manager, it's my duty to handle the shipping and returns of all orders. I ensure shipments, so long as they're ready, are sent out by the deadline. I follow up with customers to make sure they receive their orders. I ensure that large shipments don't overlap by setting deadlines that don't conflict."

"Can I interrupt?" Sean smoothly interjected. Everyone turned to look at him.

"I'm planning. Shouldn't I be the one who sets production and shipment deadlines? And then send them out to all of you?" Sean said.

"I have to set dates too," Bradley chimed in. "Production gets due dates constantly that we can't handle with our current workload. I have to make changes."

"What's the point of my job if you and Gia are constantly changing dates I put down?" Sean protested.

Surprised by Sean's tone, Jeremy asked, "Is this an ongoing issue, Sean?"

"You bet it is. I set dates in the plans, and then all the changes start. I can't keep track of them," he replied.

Jeremy knew they had other gray areas to get on the table, so he said, "That's definitely a gray area. You're all trying to do the same job." He wrote "Setting Deadlines" on a flip chart and listed Sean, Gia, and Bradley's names beside it. Anya asked to have her name added because she established dates for suppliers. Jeremy circled Sean's name. He said, "Sean, I expect you to take the lead on resolving who should set what dates for the production and shipment of orders."

Jeremy kept going. "Let's move on. Charlie, why don't you share yours?"

Charlie read his list, which included setting quality standards for parts received from suppliers.

Immediately, Anya said, "Because my team works with suppliers, I should set quality standards for their parts."

"Because my team has to assemble them, production needs to set those standards or at least be in the loop," said Bradley with a look of concern. "That has a huge impact on my team."

Jeremy saw Anya roll her eyes. First it was Gia, and now Anya. He made a mental note to follow up.

Jeremy wrote "Set quality standards for suppliers" on the flip chart. "This is a good area for us to get clarification on, especially because quality's been a problem for us. I'm adding that to our gray area list. Charlie, you can lead that discussion.

"We have two so far." He turned to the group and said, "This confirms what I've been seeing. Everyone's trying to do parts of each other's jobs, and it's confusing. Do you see it too?"

He looked around and then pushed ahead. "Let's see if there's any more gray areas."

The others read their partially completed profiles. Three additional gray areas were added to the flip chart: supplier readiness for new parts, early warning for order quantity changes, and establishing quality standards for product shipments. He stepped back from the flip chart with the five areas and asked whether they thought progress in those areas would help the team's effectiveness. Everyone studied the list and nodded yes. Anya added, "Definitely."

"Good," Jeremy said as he turned back to the group. "I'd like those of you whose names are circled to organize meetings to iron out who has what responsibility in each gray area. That will go in your position profile. Any questions on that part?"

Seeing none, Jeremy said he wanted to have the gray areas resolved and the role descriptions completed in two weeks.

Bradley said, "That's not much time, and we're really busy."

"You've got a great start with your work today. Once you've resolved the gray areas, I think you'll find writing the profile goes fast."

The team could see the two-week deadline wasn't negotiable.

Jeremy added, "They won't be written in stone. They can be drafts. I want to make sure you have most of it done before I have my one-on-one review with each of you."

"Review? Is this a performance review?" Bradley asked. He didn't look happy, and others looked concerned too.

"No," Jeremy responded emphatically. "I want to get on the same page with each of you on your responsibilities and the outcomes of your work. I should have done that already." Looking around, he said, "I feel a little guilty that I haven't. And I want to make sure each of you is getting the right level of support from me to be successful."

There was silence. Charlie said, "That's a really different approach. It sounds good." His voice sounded unsure, like he was still trying to figure out how it would work.

Jeremy chuckled, "I hope it'll be good for all of us."

That seemed to break the ice that had formed. Everyone seemed more relaxed then.

Jeremy looked around the room. He asked, "Any questions?"

"This is going to take a lot of work," Bradley said. "What about our other priorities?"

"I agree. My action item list is overfull now," Anya said. "But I see the gray areas like we've discussed. It'd be good to know who's doing what."

Several others nodded. Jeremy realized there were conflicting views. He resisted the urge to tell them to just go along and do it. Instead, he said, "I know everyone's in overload. I don't want you to labor over these profiles. I just want you to take a few minutes and document your most important responsibilities enough so we can have a good discussion."

Bradley said, "Okay. But I don't want anything I missed to end up in my year-end performance review."

Jeremy quickly held up his hand and said, "I pledge to you it won't."

Gia asked with a grin, "Were you a Boy Scout or something?"

Jeremy laughed and said, "Yes, I was. If you want, I can bring my merit badges in and show you."

Immediately, the table erupted in loud groans and Gia said, "Thanks, you don't need to."

Jeremy laughed. "I'm planning to meet with each of you individually to go over your profile. Then, we'll meet as a team two weeks from today and review everyone's job profile."

Follow Up with Anya

Jeremy concluded the meeting, and everyone gathered their things to leave. Jeremy asked Anya to stay for a minute.

With a look of concern, she asked, "Sure, is something wrong?"

He paused for a moment, heeding Sasha's advice. "No. I just want to follow up on your earlier question about your employees. It sounds like you're worried they won't be successful in their jobs."

She said, "I want to think about what you said. My two buyers are good, but they're just so new to their jobs. I may need someone with a track record of holding suppliers accountable."

"That's a good observation. I saw that when I met with you and your buyer last week."

"I haven't made any final decisions," she said. "I want to think about what I need from both of them first." She smiled. "I may have them write their position profiles."

Jeremy was glad to see she was smiling. "That works, but let's talk about this more when we review your position profile. Now, though, I'm changing topics. When Bradley said he wanted to be included in the gray area discussion, you rolled your eyes. I saw it, and he did too. It cast a negative tone to the discussion. What about his request didn't work for you?"

A look of frustration crossed her face. "He attacks me and my team. He blames us for so many issues. A lot aren't even my responsibility."

"That's why these gray area discussions are so important. I've talked to him about his approach too. I know he's frustrated because his team has to deal with all the parts issues."

"It doesn't help the situation when he jumps all over me," she said.

"That can be challenging. But I'd really like to see you and him working better together. If you can work well together, this team would be so much stronger."

"We'll see how it goes with this gray area work. And I won't roll my eyes," she said.

"Good. I really value what you do for our team, and I think you can make the change."

She left the conference room. As Jeremy was packing up his laptop and notes, he thought to himself that Charlie, Anya, and Bradley working through supplier quality issues could be a breakthrough or a disaster. He'd keep his fingers crossed.

Later in the week, Jeremy checked in with his staff on their gray area discussions. They were all following up except for Sean. Jeremy stopped by his desk to remind him.

Gia had accepted the extra work of looking at shipments that were two to four weeks from their due dates. She and Jeremy had talked about the opportunity to get exposure to other groups in All Pro, including sales and engineering. She was excited by the prospect.

By the end of the following week, everyone except Sean had their position profiles ready for their one-on-one discussion the next week. Sean was still working on his.

Reviewing Bradley's Position Profile

Jeremy's first one-on-one meeting was with Bradley on Monday morning. Jeremy needed this meeting to go well. He could see Bradley was not looking forward to their discussion when he walked into Jeremy's office.

Jeremy said, "Before we get started on your role description, I'd like to find out more about you and your career. What's important to you going forward?"

Bradley looked surprised by Jeremy's approach and paused momentarily. "Well, I've been the production manager for five years. I'm not looking for a promotion. This job is challenging enough. For the most part, I like what I'm doing. I like seeing good products come off the line and knowing my team made them. That's important to me. If I can't do that, I shouldn't be in the job."

Jeremy nodded in agreement. "It's rewarding to see shipments go out. And I know you're getting frustrated by the issues we've been having and the new Symmetry goals."

Bradley nodded and said, "You bet. When I started in this job five years ago, we had issues, but it seemed manageable. Now, I don't see a path to success."

"Bradley, I don't have the answers right now either. But I do know that if we can get the team on track, our chances go way up. And one of the steps I need to take is to make sure I know what your responsibilities are and to get agreement on the results we need. I also need to know how I can help you to be successful." He looked to see if Bradley was buying into what he was saying, but his expression didn't change. So Jeremy went on. "Let's go through your position profile."

They walked through his profile. His list of responsibilities was long and mirrored many of Jeremy's. One responsibility was "to oversee production of high-quality parts to meet shipment deadlines." His expected results were to produce parts with a 99 percent quality level and meet the customer ship date 98 percent of the time in Q4. These were the same as Jeremy's listed results and the Symmetry mandate.

Jeremy sat back and said, "This is a very thorough list. I'm guessing the quality and on-time delivery responsibilities are the most challenging. I know they are for me."

"Yes, I don't know how I'm going to deliver those at this point."

"What's going to get in the way of those that I can help with?" Jeremy asked.

"As I said before, everyone else on the team has to do their jobs so my team can produce quality parts on time. I need good parts, an error-free production plan, and a reliable quality system to make my numbers."

Jeremy nodded in agreement as he took notes.

Bradley went on. "We also need to upgrade the production line. We haven't invested enough in our equipment and it's breaking down. A lot. And then, when we make repairs to ship parts, we get written up for going over budget. We don't have priorities because everything is a priority. On-time delivery, quality, overhead spending. Everything. I need you to set priorities."

He saw Jeremy scribbling notes and added, "I've sent proposals for equipment upgrades or replacements to the last two manufacturing managers. Both were turned down. How can I keep production going with equipment that's worn out?"

Jeremy was surprised. "This is the first time I've heard about these proposals." Ken hadn't mentioned them. "And I think our priorities are clear. Delivering quality parts on time is our number one priority. I'd like to go over those proposals with you. Then, I'll take them to Ken to talk about funding them. I'm wondering if he ever saw them. He's tough but reasonable."

Bradley looked at him and smiled for the first time. "That'd be great."

Jeremy picked up Bradley's position profile. "There is one responsibility I think you missed."

Bradley raised his eyebrows. "What's that?"

Jeremy said, "Everything on your list is focused internally on your own team and getting product out the door. That's critical. I see one of your other responsibilities, as a member of my staff, is to develop positive and productive relationships with your peers on my staff."

"If you're talking about my conversation with Anya, I apologized to her and I think she and I are fine now. Our gray area discussions have gone really well in fact."

"Thank you for apologizing and the gray area work. Those are great. You have a critical role on the team with your position, experience, and judgment. You have a huge influence on the others on the team. Do you see that?" Jeremy asked.

Bradley thought for a moment. "I guess I hadn't thought about it, but you're probably right."

"If there's one recommendation I'd make on your results, it'd be to focus on developing and maintaining positive relationships."

"I know it's important. I just don't focus on it."

Jeremy smiled and said, "Yes, you and I have some similarities. I tend to do the same thing. You talked about investing in equipment. This is about investing in our team."

"Agreed." Bradley's response was short, but Jeremy could see he accepted Jeremy's feedback.

Looking at Bradley's position profile again, Jeremy said, "I don't see that you need a lot of my direction or even coaching. I do want to check in with you, so we'll have regular one-on-one meetings. Maybe every two weeks. What do you think?"

"That'll work."

"In the meantime, please check with me if there is a problem or you think our priorities aren't clear. I also want to review those proposals you wrote to upgrade the line. Can you send those to me?"

Bradley said, "Definitely." Then, glancing at his watch, he said, "I've got to get down to a meeting with my leads. Are we done?"

Jeremy smiled. "Yes, this has been really helpful for me. I appreciate that you get products out on time, even with all the stuff that happens. I mean it. Let's follow up next week on your proposals for the line."

Bradley stood up and said, "Thanks, Jeremy. I can't tell you how good this meeting has been for me. It's been a while since I've felt heard and valued around here." He walked out with a smile.

Jeremy felt relieved and much better about Bradley staying on the team. One meeting down and four to go.

The Other Position Profile Discussions

Jeremy followed the same approach in his other one-on-one meetings that week. He made sure he asked what was important to his staff members and their careers. He carefully reviewed their responsibilities and the results they were expected to deliver. They discussed how he could support their success.

Gia confirmed her career was important to her and that she'd like to look at moving into another department in All Pro in a year or so. Jeremy expressed his confidence in her abilities to fulfill her own responsibilities. He shared that her work on assessing shipments two to four weeks out would give her visibility in other departments. After reviewing her responsibilities and discussing the minimal level of support she needed from Jeremy, they agreed to have one-on-one meetings every two weeks so they could check in. Like Bradley, she said she found the meeting to be very motivating.

His one-on-one meeting with Anya was more challenging. Like Bradley, Anya was guarded at the start of the meeting. Jeremy assumed it was due to the ongoing quality issues in procurement. He started with the question of what was important to her. She told him schedule flexibility was really important to her. Being a single mom, she had sole responsibility for getting her son, Noah, to and from day care along with the myriad of other parental responsibilities. When he asked how he could help, she said she needed to leave promptly at five every day, quickly adding that she would be available from home after six for important calls or emails.

When they discussed her responsibilities and expected results, a look of disappointment crossed her face. She looked straight at Jeremy and said, "I know we have some big gaps between our actual versus expected results for supplier quality, and that's causing issues for manufacturing."

Nodding, Jeremy replied, "It is. We need action to close that gap. Do you have a plan?"

She said, "I'm working on it. When I met with Charlie and Bradley to discuss our gray area, supplier quality, they offered recommendations. I need time to fully implement them given the number of suppliers we have." She paused, looking at Jeremy.

"How long do you think that'll take?" Jeremy asked.

"It's my top priority, but probably three months. We'll have to put the documentation together and meet with suppliers. We'll need to rewrite contracts. And we'll need to hold our suppliers accountable. When we talked a couple of weeks ago, I'd said I'd look at my buyers to see if I have the staff I need to be successful. I don't. My team needs a more experienced buyer. Someone with the ability to manage a large number of suppliers and still hold them accountable. My two buyers just can't do that. At least not yet. They don't have enough experience. I'm working on the position profile for what I need."

"Would you want to replace one of the two, or do you think you need a third buyer? I'm not sure I can get an additional headcount from Ken."

"Ideally, it'd be a third buyer given the number of suppliers we have. That third buyer could give the other two guidance. I'd include that in the position profile."

She had a good point, and Jeremy had seen firsthand how inexperienced her buyers were. "I agree. Send me a summary of the position along with the cost, and I'll take it to Ken."

"Thanks, Jeremy." She took a deep breath. Looking at him directly, she said, "Jeremy, I have to admit, I'm struggling in this job. I don't have a lot of procurement experience either, and I'm new to management."

He said, "An experienced buyer will help. I can help too, although I don't have a strong procurement background. I dealt with suppliers when I was in engineering. I'd like to schedule regular one-hour meetings with you once a week."

"That'd be good."

"I hope you know you can always stop by my desk or text me or call me."

"I appreciate that."

He said, "Good. I'll follow up. Is there anything else you want to talk about?"

"I can't think of anything right now. This has been a good discussion, Jeremy. I'll get that proposal for the third buyer to you. And I really appreciate your asking what's important to me."

When Jeremy met with Charlie, Charlie told him how important developing his quality expertise was to him. Since taking over quality three years ago, he'd taken steps to develop his knowledge by reading books, attending local networking groups, and researching topics on the Internet. Now, he wanted to become certified in quality management. Jeremy asked him to put together a proposal. He'd see if All Pro could fund his certification.

When they reviewed Charlie's position profile, Jeremy saw that Charlie's very thorough list was made up of tactical quality responsibilities. It was missing an overall strategic plan for quality. Jeremy pointed that out to Charlie.

Surprisingly, Charlie beamed when he heard that. Jeremy said, "It looks like I triggered something."

Charlie said, "You did. I'd told the last several manufacturing managers the same thing. I told them we needed to overhaul our processes and system. Our current process control system was not designed for the volume of production we're doing. And it's outdated."

"Why hasn't it been at least upgraded?"

"I lobbied for a replacement, but we couldn't afford it. So I've just been tracking our results and trying to keep a lid on quality issues. Does this open the door to rethinking how we manage quality overall?"

Jeremy smiled. "Definitely. And you'll need to add that to your responsibilities. There's a lot of work to do to hit our goals this year."

Charlie made a note and said, "I'll revise my role description and send it to you later today. That'll be the first responsibility on my list." Charlie seemed satisfied with the meeting as he left Jeremy's office.

Jeremy felt good about the discussions he had had so far. He had just one more meeting to go, which would be difficult: Sean.

Sean's Decision

The meeting to review Sean's position plan was scheduled for 3:00 p.m. on Monday afternoon. Sean was on time for once.

After Sean sat down across from Jeremy, Jeremy asked, "Did you finish your position profile?"

Sean said, "No, but I've got something to share."

Surprised, Jeremy said, "Okay. What's that?"

"I'm giving my two weeks' notice. I'm quitting," he said in a mild but determined voice.

Surprised, Jeremy stared at Sean for a moment. He was at a loss for words. Then he asked, "You're quitting? Why?"

Sean fidgeted in his chair. "When you told us we needed to write our position profile and I was writing down my responsibilities, I realized I don't like most of my work. I don't like sitting at my desk and doing spreadsheets most of the day. And I'm not very good at it." He paused for a minute and continued, "When you said one of your responsibilities was to make sure you had employees who could deliver results that would make the team successful, I knew that wasn't me. That hit home."

Inwardly, Jeremy was relieved by Sean's decision. Feeling a little guilty that he was happy Sean was leaving, Jeremy masked his emotions and said, "Okay. What are your plans, then? What are you going to do?"

Sean took a deep breath. "I talked to my girlfriend last night, and

I've decided to go back to school and get a master's degree in communications." He handed an envelope to Jeremy. "This is my letter of resignation."

Still recovering from the surprise of Sean's news, Jeremy said, "Okay. I think communications is a good area for you."

With a look of relief on his face, Sean said, "I feel like a weight's been lifted off my shoulders."

Then, they discussed how to tell the staff. Jeremy asked Sean not to attend the staff meeting the next day because Jeremy and his team would need to discuss hiring Sean's replacement. Sean agreed and said he'd clean up his files and work with somebody to transition his most critical work.

They shook hands. Sean then walked out the door, texting as he went.

After Sean left, Jeremy stopped by Ken's office to tell him about Sean's resignation. Ken wasn't surprised. Jeremy had been keeping him up to date. "I'm glad he quit, but I'm concerned about what this means for your team. You've got a lot of improvement you need to make this year. You're going to have to get the new person up to speed, fast." He started typing on his computer. "I'll let Richard know about the termination. Go ahead and open a job posting."

Jeremy needed a great replacement for Sean, and quickly. He'd never hired anybody before, and he didn't want to make another hiring mistake, like Sean had been. It was time to go back to Josephine to get her advice.

Team Discusses Position Profiles and Replacing Sean

Everyone was on time for the staff meeting on Tuesday afternoon. Glancing around the room, Gia asked if Jeremy wanted her to text Sean and remind him of the meeting.

Jeremy thanked her and said, "No. I have news about Sean." That got everyone's attention.

Jeremy calmly looked around the table and said, "Sean resigned yesterday afternoon."

Reactions were mixed. Anya and Charlie looked shocked. Gia and Bradley raised their eyebrows, and Jeremy thought he saw a look of satisfaction on Gia's face. He continued, "I know that's a surprise. He gave two weeks' notice, and he's going to continue to work on his plans." He looked at his staff. "That's going to leave us short-handed until we hire a replacement and get him or her up to speed. Charlie, you used to do the job. Can you step into the role and keep the plans going while we backfill that position?"

Charlie nodded and said, "Yes, I can for a while, although, with these new goals, I'm really concerned about getting quality on track."

Jeremy said, "Thanks, and I understand your concern. That's why we'll get a great replacement in as quickly as we can." Then he asked the rest of the staff to support Charlie while they were in transition. Everyone nodded in agreement.

Jeremy then said, "I still want us to review everyone's position profile today. Last night, I put one together for the planner position, so I'd like your input because it'll be the basis for our hiring."

With that, he asked Anya to start their review of their respective position profiles. There were some clarifying questions asked, but they'd done the hard work on the gray areas outside of the staff meetings; there was little disagreement with any of the descriptions. They spent the most time on the position profile for the planning position.

After that discussion, Anya told Jeremy and the group she was glad they'd gone through the exercise of sharing their position profiles. She now had a much better idea of what each of them did. Bradley even chimed in with his agreement. He said it had been helpful even though he went in thinking it would be a waste of time.

Jeremy thanked them all again. It was gratifying to get their positive feedback.

He then said they needed to get the planning position filled within three weeks. He saw looks of disbelief on everyone's faces. He asked Anya, Bradley, and Charlie to participate in the interview team. Gia was excused because she had a vacation planned and her interaction with the role was more limited.

Jeremy wasn't sure if it was the sharing of role descriptions or the fact that they were going to have a new planner that had lifted the mood of the group, but it didn't matter. He thought people seemed to be able to joke with each other. He had mixed feelings. It would be a crazy three weeks coming up, but he liked the team's direction. On the other hand, he'd never hired anyone before, and he and the team needed a great hire.

Hiring School with Josephine

Jeremy met Josephine at 7:30 a.m. Thursday morning. He said, "I want to fill you in on the last two weeks. For the most part, the work to clarify roles has been great. But I need to replace Sean. Quickly."

She said, "Okay, getting the right people on board is critical to your success. So, what do you know about making a good hire?"

He replied, "Not a lot. I've never hired anyone before. I've interviewed candidates, but I don't think the hiring managers ever took my feedback into consideration." He paused and then said, "I've seen some bad hires. Bradley said Sean was hired because he could talk college football all day with the previous manufacturing manager."

Josephine laughed and said, "That happens a lot. Managers often make their decision based on first impressions or on how well they like the person. A bad hire is costly, but a great hire can make everyone else on the team better."

"Can you ever guarantee that you'll make a great hire?" Jeremy asked.

She replied in her soft Southern drawl, "There are never guarantees when you talk about people. But you can definitely improve your odds."

She told him to open his notebook, and then she described what she called "performance-based hiring." It was based on a process developed by Lou Adler. Then, she described the approach and key components.

She said the approach was to base the hire on the person's past performance. That was the best way to predict future performance.

She asked if he had a position profile for the job. Jeremy confirmed he did. She said, "Good. It's the foundation throughout the hiring and onboarding process. You need to clearly define what you expect a top performer to achieve in the role."

Jeremy said, "Okay," and added that to his growing list. Then he asked, "What about candidates? I'll have to figure out where to place ads."

"You can place ads. But I've made some of my best hires through networking," she said.

"Good idea. I'll reach out and ask Ken to do the same," he said, adding a reminder to his notebook. He looked up then, thinking about the challenges of figuring out how to separate the good candidates from the rest of the pack. "And then what? How do you identify good candidates? I don't want another Sean."

"Look for candidates who look like they've been successful in similar positions. Even if they're less experienced. When you have three or four good candidates, set up in-depth interviews with several of your staff. You and your staff should focus on the candidates' past accomplishments. Have them probe on not just what they did but how they did it. Have them dig in for specific examples. It's hard to fake somebody out when you have to provide very specific answers."

"These are great," Jeremy said as he took quick notes. "I feel better about hiring now."

"We aren't quite done," Josephine said. "When you and the team are making your decision, use real evidence. Too often, I've seen hiring managers swayed by a great first impression. Require real information from yourself and others as you make your decisions."

And then she said, "And don't forget, you'll need to sell a great candidate on why he or she should work for you and All Pro."

Jeremy said, shaking his head, "You're right. We may not have the best reputation out there."

"Of course, work closely with your HR team. They'll help you stay legal and follow the administrative processes," Josephine said. He nodded that he understood.

Josephine looked at the front counter and said, "I have to go. Are you all set?"

Jeremy sighed and said, "I think so."

Seeing his reaction, Josephine said, "Do your work and follow the process. You'll make a great hire."

Sunday morning, Jeremy posted the job on Indeed.com and sent the role description to his contacts on LinkedIn and Outlook. I need to update my LinkedIn profile, he thought. Especially if I can't turn things around in manufacturing.

Identifying and Choosing a Great Candidate

By the following Wednesday, Jeremy had a number of potential candidates. Most weren't a great fit, but six rose to the top of the heap. Four had come in via networking and two through the ad on Indeed.com.

Jeremy called all six candidates and narrowed the list down to three.

He met with his hiring team and shared Josephine's hiring process. They split up who'd focus on what areas and agreed to document their questions and keep good notes on the candidates' responses. Finally, they reviewed the résumés of the top three candidates.

"This is going to be hard. Good going, Jeremy," Anya said.

Individual interviews went smoothly on Monday and Tuesday of the next week. On Wednesday morning, the interview team members met to score the three candidates. They went through each candidate and summarized his or her answers. Jeremy had them score the candidates high, medium, or low on five different areas: skills match, documented results, teamwork, communication, and coachability.

Candidate 1, Michael, scored high on communication; medium on skills, coachability, and teamwork; and low on documented results. When pressed for specific numbers and time frames, he couldn't provide concrete answers.

Candidate 2, Susan, scored high on skills, medium on communication and results, and low on coachability and teamwork. When pushed on how she achieved results, she sounded like the Lone Ranger in solving problems on her own and without any help, even from her manager.

Candidate 3, Aaron, scored high on communication, teamwork, and coachability and medium on skills and results. He gave concrete examples of each area, including how he had communicated status updates on a large project in college to keep everyone in the loop. He had attributes of a top performer. The team's reservations were due to his lack of experience and his youthful age. He was only two years out of college. Still, he'd had great results in a similar, although more junior, role at another company.

"He's about the same age as Sean, but he seems extremely capable to me," Bradley said. "I liked his answers. He gave credit where it was due, and I think I could trust him with communicating with me before he changes dates whenever he feels like."

"Do you get the feeling Aaron could get up to speed quickly and get in the game as soon as possible?" Jeremy asked. This concerned him a little; Aaron didn't have nearly as much experience as the others did.

"I think so," Anya said after a moment of collective silence. "It's a bit of a risk, but there's a risk with all of them. The projects he headed in school sounded like a lot of responsibility. He did those while also working part time."

Charlie added, "He has good experience working with complex Excel models from his finance classes. He demonstrated that with the work he's doing in his current job. When I probed, he had specific solutions he had used in other spreadsheets that would eliminate the errors in the planning spreadsheets Sean was using."

"Do we agree? Aaron is our top candidate?" Jeremy asked.

Everyone chimed in that they agreed.

Jeremy called Aaron's references. They were glowing. One professor said Aaron would make any team better. Jeremy was convinced Aaron would be a great addition, if Jeremy could convince him to accept.

Convincing Aaron to Enlist

Jeremy called Aaron to ask him to meet at Roast on Friday morning at seven. Aaron was already there when Jeremy walked in. He looks really young, Jeremy thought. Jeremy reminded himself that appearance didn't matter. Aaron had demonstrated great performance in school and his current job.

Josephine saw Jeremy come in and pointed to herself with a questioning look. Jeremy smiled and shook his head no. She smiled in return when she saw him shake hands with Aaron and direct him over to "their" booth. She returned to the counter.

Aaron was clearly nervous as he sat down across from Jeremy. Jeremy started by saying, "Thanks for meeting me so early, Aaron. We'd like to offer you our planning position. We think you'd be a great addition to our team."

Aaron looked relieved. He smiled and said, "Thanks. That's great news. I'm really excited about the position."

Jeremy laughed and said, "You'd be our only planner, and we really depend on this position. For you, it's a solid promotion, and that's how others would see it."

Aaron nodded that he understood. Jeremy said, "I know we discussed most of the responsibilities and expectations for this position, but I want to run through the position profile again so that we're aligned." He handed Aaron a copy, and they walked through it line by line.

Aaron told Jeremy he appreciated seeing the complete document. Then he asked, "I understand the previous guy, Sean, wasn't successful in this job. Can you tell me why?" He paused for a moment before adding, "I'm concerned about why and if I'll have the same issues."

At first, Jeremy was taken aback by Aaron's directness, but he was glad that Aaron had asked. Jeremy said, "Good, I don't want you to be surprised." Then, he walked through the top issues with the position. He said he was confident Aaron could fix the spreadsheet errors that Sean had made and also get plans out on time. He said he thought the most challenging part of the job would be dealing with the multiple demands from different areas. Some were from customers or other All Pro departments such as sales, which could be really pushy. They discussed the need for excellent communication from the position, especially when changes were made. Aaron said he would set consistent expectations with all the "customers" of the position. Jeremy thought that that was an excellent approach.

Aaron then asked about All Pro. He said that he'd heard the company was falling behind. It had a reputation of not being progressive and was losing business to other companies. Jeremy acknowledged the market had become more competitive. Then he talked about his goal of building a strong team to help ensure All Pro would again be the leader in the market. He said his focus was on both the business and the employees. He finished by saying, "We need a strong planner. Someone who can really handle multiple demands and deliver excellent plans. Those plans drive our output and enable us to meet our customers' needs."

It was an intense discussion. Jeremy paused for a moment and, leaning forward, said, "I'd like to have you on our team." Then he walked through the details of the offer.

Aaron was listening intently and taking a few notes. He then looked up and, breaking into a broad smile, he said, "I'd like to accept the position."

"Great," Jeremy said.

Aaron quickly added, "I'll need to give notice when I get in to work today. I'm hoping two weeks will be enough."

Jeremy said, "That will work for me. Just let me know."

Jeremy said he'd send Aaron the offer letter and would need Aaron to return a signed copy. They stood up to leave and shook hands. Both were beaming.

Jeremy was just walking out when he caught Josephine's eye. She was obviously busy, so he smiled and gave her a thumbs up. She smiled back.

Later that day, as Jeremy was planning the rest of his week, he blocked time on his calendar to meet with Aaron every day. He wanted to get Aaron up to speed quickly. He felt better now about his team. He'd just replaced a weak link with a strong link.

The first quarter ended that day, March 31. He and his team hadn't hit their original Q1 goals, and they were lightyears away from hitting Symmetry's mandate by end of the year. He didn't have any time to waste in getting Aaron and the team up to speed as quickly as possible. He was meeting Josephine the next morning at Roast. He wanted to run some ideas by her on getting his team fully engaged.

STEP 3

Build Commitment and Accountability

Saturday, April 1

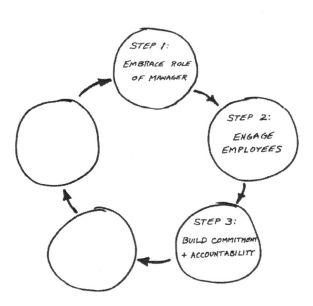

Josephine and Jeremy Discuss Commitment and Accountability

Jeremy was at Roast bright and early Saturday morning with his latte in hand when Josephine joined him in their booth. It was quiet. Jeremy filled Josephine in on the previous three weeks.

She said, "It sounds like the role discussions went well at the team level and individually too."

"It did. Your recommendation to have my staff members figure out the gray areas was brilliant. They had to work through the different pieces. It seems like they're more at ease with each other. And I think Aaron's going to be a great addition. Thanks for your process and ideas."

"You're welcome. You know the next month is critical in getting him up to speed quickly."

Jeremy nodded. "Definitely. That's one of my top priorities. Charlie's agreed to mentor him because he used to do the role. I've also blocked time in my schedule to meet with him every day for his first week." He paused for a moment, chuckling. "Last night, Aaron actually sent me his own ideas on the position, and he hasn't even started yet. He's so positive."

Josephine chuckled and said, "Wow. You have a go-getter on your hands."

"Yep. Now, I want to build on the team's improvement. And quickly. We're not going to meet our Q1 goals, so the pressure's just going to get more intense."

"I think you've laid a great foundation, Jeremy. You've had quality individual conversations that have built trust between you and your employees. Everyone knows his or her role and what's expected, and you've made a great hire with Aaron. Next is step 3, where you get commitment to the team and the business. That's going to make a huge difference."

"What do you recommend?"

"Commitment to the team is based on trust within the team. So you accelerate building trust."

"That sounds good, but I always thought that just takes time."

"Time helps, but you can accelerate it. As I said before, people tend to trust people they know. So, help them get to know each other more quickly. And then have them discuss how they want to work together."

"Have you done this with other teams?" He was having trouble seeing how to do that.

"You bet. You have people get to know each other by having them share information about themselves. Like, where they're from, their family, who's important to them, and so forth. People don't often share that type of information. There's not enough time, or it seems too personal."

Jeremy thought about his team. "I think some people would love that and others not so much."

Josephine laughed. "That's what you'd think. But I've found even the biggest doubters say it's a good activity. It will develop stronger relationships. You can also have people share what they think their strengths are, and their weaknesses too. You've done that, and I think you saw that it helped."

He added notes in his notebook. "It did. I think that'd be great if they'd do it."

"A lot will depend on how you present it. I think you'll be surprised by their willingness once they get over the request itself. Then, to sustain those relationships, you need to remind people of how they want to work together."

Jeremy looked up from writing notes in his notebook and asked, "How do you do that?"

"I have the team develop team rules on how they want to work together. But then, if you go that route, just make sure you use the rules. It's easy to be nice to each other and make promises when you're in a meeting talking about relationships. You have to hold everyone accountable for following the rules, especially when things go haywire," she said.

"That all makes sense, especially for accountability on how we work. What about getting commitment to the business?"

"Good employees commit to the business when they believe in its purpose and direction and see their role in the success of the business."

Jeremy immediately added, "And when they think the business can be successful. I need some breakthrough strategies. We aren't making much headway in improving our results." He was feeling the weight of Q1's failure.

"I agree. First, though, you need the team aligned to the business. So, before you jump directly to strategies, I'd recommend you develop a mission and vision with the team. Get your team involved in developing them."

"Developing a mission and vision will take time, and I don't know how they'd add any value." He'd said that in a rush, and he felt a little guilty about just dumping it all out in the open.

She looked at him for a second before saying, "All right. We can skip them, but do you want to hear why I think you should do them?"

"Yes." His reply didn't have a lot of heart.

She laughed. "That wasn't very enthusiastic. A mission and vision that are shared across the team provide clear guidance and direction for the team. If you involve the team in developing them, the vision will inspire the team. And it'll help unify them. Get them out of their silos, which is where they've gone when things haven't gone well. Right?"

"Yes, they have. And that's when the finger pointing happens."

She knowingly shook her head. "I do think you have to be careful to make this not just about Symmetry and what Symmetry wants. You'll get more buy-in to go after those tough goals if it's what the *team* aspires to." She'd put emphasis on the word "team."

Jeremy had to admit she was right. "I see your point. It'd be great to reference that common mission and vision." He pulled out his notebook. "Any recommendations on how to develop the mission and vision quickly? When I've done them, it's been tedious."

"Start with some good, motivating examples of missions and visions. Then have the group brainstorm elements they think should be included. I always had good luck with pairing people up and having each pair develop a draft mission or vision statement. Don't give them much time. Have the pairs share their statements, and then have new pairs develop another version. It keeps it moving, and no one is married to any one mission or vision. It stops a lot of the wordsmithing that makes it tedious, if you know what I mean."

"I do," Jeremy said quickly, thinking back to his first company's offsite. The group's development of a vision had taken forever, and the result had been a bland compromise that no one could get behind.

"Make sure you get buy-in on how the team's going to use them.

That will save you a lot of time and energy in the long run because it'll help with decisions," she added.

As he made a note in his notebook, he asked, "What about coming up with strategies? I really need some breakthrough strategies. What have you seen work, especially with impossible goals?" he asked.

Shaking her head, she said, "First thing, you can't go in saying they're impossible. You need to reframe it in your own head as something that's challenging but not impossible. Otherwise, aren't you setting yourself and the team up for failure? With your style, you tend to see all the negatives and obstacles." Her Southern drawl softened the hard observation she'd made.

He grimaced. "You caught me. I won't say impossible."

"Good," she said. "To get the breakthrough strategies you need, you have to get your whole team's input. I usually do brainstorming to surface ideas. Make sure everyone has a chance to contribute. Then you'll have to get them down to a manageable number."

"That's a good idea," Jeremy said. He added that to his notes.

"Once you have your few key strategies, cascade the team strategies and goals down to your staff. Their individual goals need to be aligned to the team goals, and their goals should be SMART. Do you know what I mean by SMART?"

He nodded. "Specific, measurable, action oriented, realistic, and time based."

"It's easy for accountability to get lost in all the detail. Just make sure you have one person who's responsible for each significant strategy. Make them the owner, and have them hold others accountable. You can't manage this all yourself."

Before working with Josephine, he might have denied that. Now, he appreciated her wisdom. "Good advice. You're probably right about my not being able to manage everything."

He looked at all his notes from their meeting. "I'm concerned about getting through all this. It's going to take forever to get through building both team and business commitment. Those are going to be intense discussions."

"It helps to get away. I'd recommend you do it all at an offsite. In one fell swoop. I've done it over two days. You get so much done, and just spending time together will further build trust and teamwork."

He hadn't thought about that, but he liked the idea. "That would be good given where we are right now."

"I agree." Josephine began to pick up her things at the table. "I have to go. You should think about it. There are some great little places not far away where you can get meeting space that's reasonable."

He said, "I'll look around. Thanks, Josephine." He cleared his coffee cup and packed up his backpack.

Over the weekend, Jeremy developed an agenda for a two-day offsite. It included everything Josephine had described. He included the personal sharing exercise that Josephine had recommended after realizing he himself knew very little about his employees from a personal standpoint. He found a great location called Grand Lake Resort. It fit the bill with a relaxing resort feel, but also with a functional conference room. He scheduled the offsite for Thursday and Friday, April 20 and 21, the week that Aaron would start as the planner. Now he just needed to get his team to buy in.

The Team Learns about the Offsite, and Aaron Starts

At staff on Tuesday afternoon, Jeremy said he had a surprise for the team. Anya said, "You've just been full of surprises." Everyone laughed. It started the discussion on a good note.

Jeremy told the team, "I feel we've been making good progress as a team. I feel like I've gotten to know each of you better." He saw nods from everyone on staff. He continued, "I feel everyone knows their own role and everyone else's role. We're beginning to see the benefits of ironing out our gray areas, especially in quality. And we have a great hire starting next Monday." Again, everyone nodded.

He paused before starting again. "We just finished Q1 and our performance improved during the quarter. But, we didn't hit our goals. I appreciate your hard work. It's taking herculean effort to make those improvements. From my perspective, it feels like we're always in fire-fighting mode. And it's stressful. I'd like us to get out of that." Looking around, he asked, "Do any of you feel that way too?"

Gia and Charlie quietly nodded in agreement. Anya and Bradley were quiet too until Bradley said, "Yeah. I feel it. Like, every day. My team takes the brunt of it because we have to actually make all the parts and have to deal with all the issues."

Anya, in a defensive tone, said, "Well, if you mean bad parts when you say 'issues,' my team does the best we can. We have to deal with a lot of issues, too." She sat back and crossed her arms.

Jeremy hadn't intended to get into a long discussion about the off-site. It felt like the team was suddenly going backwards. He said, "This discussion is a symptom of being in firefighting mode. It's hard on the business, and it's hard on our teamwork." He glanced at Anya and Brad-ley. "To hit our numbers and not kill each other, we need breakthrough strategies and to improve how we work together. So, to speed those up, we're having a two-day staff meeting on Thursday and Friday, April 20 and 21, at Grand Lake Resort. It's a bit of a drive. I've reserved rooms for all of us to stay overnight on the 20th. Ken has approved paying for the rooms and all the meals. We'll focus on teamwork and the business. Aaron starts that Monday, so it'll help integrate him into our team." He paused for a moment. Everyone was surprised, even shocked.

Bradley spoke first. "Two days? That's a lot of time away from the office." Charlie nodded in agreement.

Looking at her calendar on her laptop, Anya added, "I have a vendor coming in on that Friday. They've been hard to schedule. And I'll have to make arrangements for Noah. Maybe with my mom."

"I understand some of you will need to reschedule meetings and so forth. But there's never going to be a perfect time when everyone's free and there aren't issues at the office. My top priority right now is to get our team to the next level. I'm telling you about the offsite today so you can make arrangements. I expect all of you to attend."

He saw his staff make notes to change their plans.

He asked Gia to stay after the meeting. "We need some data for the offsite on our shipments in Q1. I'd like to know how many shipments were on time and how many were late. For the late ones, I'd like to know why. For example, did customers make changes to orders, or did we have problems with our suppliers? Also, if we have it, I'd like info on the quality of our shipments. Would you have time to put that together?"

Gia said, "Yes. I'll work with my team to pull that together. I'll need to have several people work overtime to pull data and reports."

Jeremy smiled and said, "I'll pay for that. I know you'll manage their overtime."

"I'll have it for the offsite." Then she turned and walked out.

Aaron started the next Monday and immediately jumped in with both feet. Jeremy had put together a thorough onboarding plan with input from his staff. He tried to balance the boring "fill out all the paperwork" activities with meetings with Jeremy and the staff.

Jeremy noted that Tuesday's staff meeting was more upbeat. Aaron brought a positive and energetic vibe to the meeting, along with a lot of questions.

By Wednesday, Aaron was beginning to take over some of the planning spreadsheets that Charlie was completing. He'd already implemented several changes to catch errors and was meeting with key stakeholders. Jeremy met with Aaron Wednesday morning to discuss his progress. It was still early, but Jeremy realized he'd need to expand Aaron's role so he'd feel challenged.

The only downside to the week was that All Pro's Q1 results had been finalized, and manufacturing was again in the spotlight. Jeremy met with Ken late Wednesday night to discuss their numbers. Ken said, "You had mixed results in Q1. Thanks to all the scrambling you did, you got Symmetry's shipments to them. And your trend line is improving. It sounds like the work you're doing to review shipments several weeks out is making a difference. But we didn't meet our revenue targets for the quarter because you couldn't get enough shipments out. I really

hope you get the breakthroughs needed at your offsite." Then he turned
back to his computer screen.

    Me too, Jeremy thought as he walked out.

The Offsite

Thursday, April 20

Committing to the Team

The Grand Lake Resort lived up to its description. The Craftsman-style lodge was on a beautiful lake rimmed with large evergreen trees. The conference room was on the second floor with a large balcony overlooking the lake. It was well equipped with a conference table, flip charts, and a digital projector. A light breakfast with coffee and orange juice was set up in the room before the team arrived. The meeting was to start at 8:00 a.m., and everyone was there by 7:45.

Once everyone had coffee and breakfast, Jeremy started. "Good morning. Thanks for clearing your schedules and driving up here. We'll be doing work today and tomorrow that'll be critical to our success as a team and the business." He paused for a moment. "I feel good about all of you on this team. I've gotten to know each of you better, and I appreciate what you bring and the work you've done to keep us on track. And I think we've added a great resource in Aaron."

Everyone glanced at Aaron. Heads were nodding in agreement.

"We all know we have some very aggressive goals to hit from Symmetry. And we didn't hit our Q1 goals. We're trending up, but we need to make some big improvements in our business to be successful. Improvements that a high-performing team can deliver. So, this morning we're going to focus on improving our teamwork. Then, this afternoon and tomorrow, we'll focus on the business. By the time we leave tomorrow, my goal is for us to have specific strategies to drive our success this year. We'll have owners for each of the strategies and what part each of us has in the strategies. It will be a busy two days." He paused to see if anyone had any concerns.

Seeing none, he started again. "Great teamwork is based on a foundation of trust. We all trust people we know professionally and personally. We're first going to get to know each other better. Any questions before we start?"

Bradley said, "Yeah. I think we know each other pretty well. We're together five days a week."

"You know each other as coworkers, as people you work with. But if we get to know each other at a deeper level, it'll shorten the time to build more trust within the team," Jeremy replied. "How well do you know each other in terms of your backgrounds?" Jeremy looked around at everyone. "For myself, I've learned more about all of you, but I can't say I know very much about your history."

Anya said, "You're right. I don't know much about any of you. Well, maybe Gia."

Bradley just shrugged his shoulders as if to say "whatever."

Hoping Bradley would come around, Jeremy continued, "This is what we're going to do. "I'm going to have you share a brief explanation of your childhood, where you grew up, your siblings, and whether you are the oldest or youngest. Also, I want you to share something from your childhood that influenced you as an adult." Then there was silence. He looked around the table, hoping someone else would start.

With a determined look on her face, Anya broke the ice and talked about growing up in her family of five in Columbus, Ohio. Jeremy asked her to talk about something from her childhood that still influenced her. She talked about her mom getting her degree while raising a large family, saying that her mom had influenced her own decision to continue her career after getting married and having a baby. She said she didn't know if everyone was aware, but she was now divorced with a three-year-old son, Noah. She said she planned to get her master's degree part time when Noah was older. She said she currently had her hands full. She got acknowledging nods from several at the table.

Aaron said, "I have a three-year-old nephew, and he's a handful. I don't know how you do it."

"Thanks. It's great some days and not some days, if you know what I mean," she said with a smile.

Aaron said, "Yep. I bet."

The others followed Anya. There were a number of commonalities. Charlie and Aaron each had grown up in families with five kids, although Charlie was the second oldest in his family and Aaron was the youngest in his. Gia and Jeremy found out they both had grown up in Pittsburgh. Gia was still a Steelers fan, whereas Jeremy had adopted the closest NFL team, the 49ers. She jokingly forgave him for it, noting that Pittsburgh had more Super Bowl rings.

Sharing who or what had most influenced them from their childhoods yielded the most amazing stories. Gia talked about her father raising her after her mom had died when she was a toddler. She said he had worked two jobs when she started grade school so she could have a better life. He'd set aside money to buy her lacrosse equipment when she was a teen and never missed one of her games. She'd gone to college on a lacrosse scholarship. She said she called him at least twice a week to share what was going on in her life and to check up on him because he was getting older. Bradley was impressed she'd played lacrosse. His son had played high school lacrosse, and he knew it was a tough sport. She smiled when he said that.

Aaron shared that one of his sisters had always wanted to move away from home and start a career. She'd died seven years ago, when he was a teenager. He said her dream had kept him on track in college and looking for opportunities away from the Phoenix area, where he had grown up.

When Bradley talked about his childhood influences, he paused for a moment. Jeremy could see he was deciding what to say. He shared that his parents had told him stories about growing up in the segregated South when there were separate bathrooms, drinking fountains, and schools. His mom had told him about a white boy, about her age, who ran up to her smiling and then shouted the "N" word at her and ran off. He said she'd warned him to be careful around people he didn't know because you never know what people will say to you because you're black. He said he thought her comments made him more reserved.

Gia said she'd had people call her names because she was Indian.

For an instant, Jeremy didn't know what to say. Then, looking at Gia and Bradley, he said, "You know, I don't like that when I see it, but it's really different when it happens to people you know. That must have been really hard. For both of you. And for your mom, Bradley."

"It was, but my parents made sure we understood it was just a small group of people. They made a point of making sure we still experienced the whole world. They dragged us to all the museums and festivals they could find. That was great until I became a teenager and it wasn't cool to go to museums." He chuckled.

Charlie spoke up then. Like Bradley, his aunt had dragged him and his siblings to all sorts of places and events too. He said he hadn't always liked it until she had taken him to Legoland, where he could enter Lego-building competitions. He shared that he liked getting every little piece in the perfect spot. Bradley chimed in that he saw that in how picky Charlie was in setting up the quality inspection equipment. That caused everyone to laugh.

Jeremy went last, saying he didn't have anything profound to share from his childhood. He couldn't wait to leave home. "My parents always argued," he said. "That was hard to be around. I'd decided I'd never get married. But then I met Sasha. I have a great relationship with her, and she helps keep me balanced." He saw several nods of understanding.

He looked around. "We didn't talk about who or what's important for each of you. Sasha is important to me. Anybody else?"

Bradley immediately jumped in and said, "My wife, Alisha, and my twenty-year-old son. He's going to school in Washington."

Anya said, "My mom and my son."

Charlie went next, saying it was the two women in his house, his wife and his mom.

Aaron spoke up then. "My parents in Arizona and my brother. I'm really close to them. Also, my girlfriend back in Arizona. We're in a long-distance relationship right now. Time will tell how it works out. It's hard to stay connected."

Everyone else had gone but Gia. She looked around, hesitating. She finally said, "My partner, Angela, is important to me. I don't think I've shared that with anybody except Anya." She glanced over at Anya, who smiled in return.

Jeremy was surprised, but he was glad that she'd shared. He had no idea that Gia had a partner. He said, "Thanks for sharing. How long have you been together?"

She said, "Two years. We've been quiet about it. Some people aren't too open to the idea."

Charlie jumped in and said, "I'm glad you told us. I never knew, and you never talk about anything outside work."

Nodding, she said, "You have no idea how hard it can be."

"Actually, none of us talks about life outside work very much. I'd like to change that, although, with my personality, I do tend to focus on work," Jeremy said with a smile.

"We know that," Anya said.

Everyone laughed. Jeremy said, "After a break, we'll talk about our strengths and weaknesses."

They walked away, each in a discussion with someone else.

Sharing Strengths and Weaknesses

The team reconvened promptly at 9:30 a.m. Jeremy started by thanking them for sharing about themselves. "Next, we're going to talk about our strengths and weaknesses and how we can leverage all of our strengths for the whole team. I can start. I actually shared my strengths and weaknesses at a staff meeting about a month ago. Aaron, you weren't there, but I shared that my strengths are being analytical, organized, and results oriented. I focus on getting things done. The downside is that sometimes I don't take care of the people side, especially when I'm stressed. I just don't realize it when I am too impersonal or I miss signs that somebody is upset. My request is for you to let me know if you're concerned or if I'm too focused on tasks." He paused then and looked around. "I don't know if anybody has any comments or questions."

Anya spoke up. "It really helped me understand you better. And I can see that you're working on it, and I really appreciate that. It makes a big difference to me. I think I am kind of the opposite."

Jeremy asked, "How so? Why don't you go next?"

"Okay," she replied. "I think I'm more people focused. I like meeting new people, and I can establish relationships really quickly and come up with opportunities. Especially for win–win situations. I think that's helped me work well with our suppliers and negotiate some good contracts. I guess on the downside, I'm not always very organized and task focused. I don't always go through the details the way I probably should."

She paused, looking around the table.

Immediately, Charlie responded, "I see that positive outgoing side of you. I know I can always count on a smile when I meet with you."

Nodding in agreement, Jeremy said, "Agreed. Any other questions or comments for Anya?" There were none.

Bradley said, "I'll go next. I'm more like Jeremy. I'm analytical and systematic in my approach. I want to know the process and details. If I don't see them, I start asking questions. Lots of questions. Some people might find that frustrating, but I need it for my job." He glanced at Anya.

She shook her head. "You do ask a lot of questions. You're so detail oriented. Sometimes, that's really challenging for me."

"Challenging? I'm not sure what you mean. Or why it would be challenging."

"Sometimes, all your questions make me think you don't trust me and my team. Or that you're just being critical. Not that procurement hasn't had issues. But sometimes, it's just too much," she said.

Bradley replied, "I just need to understand the situation and what's going to happen. Especially if it affects my team. Plus, that's just the way my mind works. I don't think about all my questions."

"I see that, but sometimes the questions are over the top. Maybe you could help me understand why you're asking and how it'll affect your team. That way, I'd know what you need instead of you just peppering me with questions. Okay?"

Bradley paused for a moment and said, "That's fair. I just need you to remind me and also think about my team too."

Anya nodded in agreement and said, "I'll try to. There's a lot I don't know about production."

Bradley said, "I can try to fill you in on production. Would you want to sit in on some of our weekly check-ins?"

"That would probably help," Anya said.

Jeremy was relieved that both seemed willing to change how they interacted. He looked at the two of them to see if there was anything else they wanted to say. They looked satisfied. He said, "It's good to get that out on the table. Thank you. Good discussion. Any other questions or concerns for Anya or Bradley?" There were none, so Jeremy asked Charlie to go next.

"I think my strengths are that I try to support others on the team. Others tell me I'm pretty evenly tempered and humble, so I'm easy to work with." He commented then, "I'm not so sure about humble."

Gia laughed and said, "That's so funny. You're just being humble in saying that."

"That is you," Bradley added, smiling at Charlie.

Charlie looked flustered for an instant, but he got it and laughed too.

"Good catch Gia," Jeremy said. "Charlie, I really value the fact that you help us stay on an even keel as a team. What about weaknesses or areas where you're not strong?"

"Sometimes I think I don't rock the boat enough. Like when a request gets turned down, I just accept it instead of pushing for it."

"So, if you bring something up and I don't see you bring it up again, it's not that you don't care. Is that the case?" Jeremy asked.

Charlie nodded in confirmation.

This concerned Jeremy. He said, "I value your judgment on situations. What should I do or we do to understand how strongly you feel about something?"

Charlie said, "Well, I own telling you if I feel that way. But you could also check with me?"

"That's good for me to know. Actually, for all of us to know," Jeremy said, looking around.

Others nodded in agreement.

Gia jumped in. "That's the opposite of me. I will push and push to get what I think's needed. I drive for results and whatever's needed to deliver them." She smiled then. "The downside of that approach is that I can alienate people because I push too hard."

Bradley said, "I have noticed when I try to negotiate with you on something, you start out so adamant, I have to decide how hard I want to push. If I push back hard enough, then you'll listen."

Charlie said, "That doesn't work very well for me."

Gia looked at both of them. "I didn't realize I was doing that. That's good to know. I am going to try to be more mindful. Let me know if I'm pushing too hard."

They both said they would.

Jeremy turned toward Aaron. "What about you and your strengths and weaknesses?"

Aaron looked around and said, "This has been an awesome discussion. I think my strengths are engaging with people. I've heard that I'm a good listener. I'm also driven to get results. But sometimes I don't say no to people, and then I overcommit and get stressed out."

"So we should watch that with you. We need to make sure we're not pushing too hard. I should work with you to make sure we're aligned on priorities," Jeremy said.

Aaron said, "That would help." He looked like he was thinking of something else. "I'm not stressed now. Don't get me wrong. I'm loving this and the work I'm doing." He said that in a rush.

Bradley laughed and said, "We'll help you get stressed out with all the changes we'll ask you to make on your plans. Believe me."

It looked like Aaron didn't know how to take Bradley's comment. Gia said, "He's kind of serious. It can get hectic."

"I understand. I'll be fine, and I'll let you know if I'm getting stressed," Aaron replied with renewed confidence.

Jeremy said, "That'll be important. Thanks for sharing, Aaron. You and I will follow up."

Aaron nodded in agreement.

Jeremy thanked everyone for pitching in. He said he valued the different strengths everyone had and that he wanted each person to bring their strengths to the team so that they could do their best work.

He could see that the high energy the team had had during the discussion was beginning to wane. He said they'd take a fifteen-minute break and reconvene at 10:30 to discuss team rules. The discussions had been helpful, but he knew everyone would forget about their agreements once they left the offsite. The rules would serve as reminders of what they'd agreed to at the offsite.

Establishing Team Rules

After their break, Jeremy started the next discussion by thanking them for their work up to this point at the offsite. "Any comments or observations on our work so far this morning?" He looked around.

Anya said, "I think it was a good discussion."

Nodding in agreement, Bradley said, "It was a good discussion. But how do we keep it up? You know, sustain it?"

Looking at Bradley, Jeremy broke into a big smile. "Thanks, Bradley. You just gave the intro for our next agenda item. I want us to agree on how we're going to work together so everyone can do their best. That's where our team rules come in."

"Team rules?" Charlie asked.

"Yes, team rules in how we want to work together and treat each other. We'll keep these in front of us. We'll start every staff meeting with a review of them. And they'll be posted in the office. They'll be visible to all manufacturing employees."

"So, these would apply to our own teams too?" Gia asked.

"I think, at a minimum, you should share them with your teams and decide if you want to adopt them or come up with your own. We can talk more about that after we develop them. You can decide what you do with them in your own group." He paused and asked, "Make sense?"

Everyone nodded in agreement. Encouraged by their reactions, he said, "I want to make sure everybody has a say. So, we're going to pair up, and each pair will come up with at least two team norms, keeping in mind the discussions this morning. Any questions?"

Not hearing any, he paired Aaron with Charlie and Anya with Bradley and said he'd work with Gia. Everyone headed off to separate places. They had twenty minutes to come up with their proposed norms. As they headed to the dock area, Gia told Jeremy that pairing Anya and Bradley was brilliant. He said, "We'll see."

After twenty minutes, everyone was back except for Anya and Bradley. Feeling apprehensive, he was just about to send Aaron to look for them when they came strolling back, smiling and talking together. Everyone looked at them expectantly.

Seeing their reaction, Anya laughed and said, "What? Did you expect me to push him into the lake or something?"

Jeremy said, "The thought crossed my mind. I'm glad to see you're both dry."

Bradley said, "We had a great discussion. We realized we both want the same things. We just come at it differently."

"That's good. Enlighten us," Jeremy said.

"Okay," Anya said. She went up to the flip chart and asked Bradley to read what he'd written. She wrote, "Assume good intentions and ask questions for clarification." She said, "We both want this as one of our rules. If we assume good intentions at the start, we can work through a lot of questions and tough issues."

Jeremy was impressed by their work. He wondered to himself if this was a breakthrough for them. He hoped so. Together, they'd be awesome.

Excited, Aaron said, "I think we had something similar. We had, 'Trust each other: when in doubt, ask for clarification and understanding.' I think that's pretty similar, but I like yours more." Charlie agreed.

So, they had their first team norm. Everyone shared the other norms they'd come up with in their pairs. Within an hour, they'd debated the different proposals from the pairs and identified five more. Be authentic and open with your ideas, information, and suggestions. Engage in healthy debate focused on ideas, not people. Voice your concerns about a topic or issue, but commit to the team's final decision. Be positive with each other. And, finally, hold each other accountable. Jeremy confided to the group that, as the manager, they might believe he was responsible for holding everyone accountable. He wanted all of them to do the same, including holding him accountable.

They voted on the list, and it was final. It was a great way to end the morning. Everyone filed out of the conference room. They were going to eat lunch together on the veranda by the restaurant. Some went to the lobby to check in to their rooms before lunch.

Lunch on the veranda at the resort was a relaxed affair. People followed up on the nuggets they'd collected that morning from sharing personal histories. Gia and Jeremy talked about their favorite Italian restaurants in Pittsburgh. Aaron, Gia, and Bradley discussed house boating on Lake Powell and then lacrosse. The entire team gave Jeremy a hard time about his need to have a detailed agenda for staff meetings. Bradley tried to come to his rescue.

Developing a Shared Mission and Vision

The team members were back in the conference room at 1:30 after lunch. They seemed refreshed and ready to start again. When Jeremy told them they were going to develop a mission and vision for the team, he got the pushback he'd expected. It was Bradley who spoke for the team. "We've done those before. It takes too long, and it's a waste of time."

Seeing that only Aaron and Anya seemed open to the idea, Jeremy said, "I can see how you'd think that, but I want us to have a common mission and vision that we all aspire to achieve. I think it's too easy to slip back into our respective silos, and we can't afford that." He could see they were thinking about it, so he quickly added, "Besides, we'll be quick about it, and, I promise you, we'll use them."

He jumped right into creating their mission statement. Jeremy explained, "Our mission statement should be simple. It should state who we are, what we do, and who we do it for." He flipped over a sheet on a flip chart to show an example of the mission statement for a nonprofit. "'United Center is a social service agency providing emergency housing assistance to low-income children and families at risk in inner-city Dallas.' This is a mission statement that clearly describes what United Center does. Any questions?"

Aaron asked, "So, this is only for our department?"

"Yes, it's just for manufacturing. Us as a team and an organization. Anything else before we start?" he asked, looking around.

Gia asked, "And this is focused on our customers, like Symmetry, right?"

Jeremy said, "Yes, it's our core reason for being from an external perspective. That's how we should look at it."

Jeremy had them break into two groups. The first group, with Gia, Charlie, and Aaron, was to come up with a statement regarding their customers. The second group, with Anya, Bradley, and himself, would describe what they do. He gave them fifteen minutes to develop two options.

The two groups came back and put their creations together. One combination resonated with the group, and it was almost their final version. "All Pro Manufacturing produces state-of-the-art electro-mechanical parts for medical, military, and high-tech equipment manufacturers."

After the combination was written on the flip chart, Jeremy looked around and asked, "Any comments? Questions? Concerns?" Hearing none and seeing satisfied looks around the table, he said, "Done. That wasn't too bad, was it? And it's just two o'clock. We'll tackle the vision after a ten-minute break. Good work."

Regrouping shortly before 2:30, Jeremy started the discussion by telling the team that a vision should describe where the team would like to be in three to five years, if the team was highly successful. It should paint a picture of their future state. He reminded them of Martin Luther King Jr.'s "I Have a Dream" speech and JFK's challenge to put a man on the moon. He said, "These visions inspired the country to great achievements and change. I am hoping ours will inspire us to achieve great results together." He looked around and then said, "And unify us as a team."

Then, he asked them to think of their vision in terms of how they meet the needs of their customers. He asked if any of them had any information about the needs of their biggest customers. He said, "For example, I read that Symmetry is planning to increase the number of products in the higher end of its product line to go after the military and health care markets. I suspect that they're finding the lower end of the market isn't profitable."

"I read that article," Charlie said. "They said they are emphasizing the quality of their products and their time to market with their customers."

"Good," Jeremy said. "What other needs do our customers have?"

"Low cost," Bradley said. "Our customers have a need for low-cost parts so they can be competitive." He was looking at Anya.

She nodded in agreement and said, "I agree. All our customers are facing ongoing pressure to lower their costs. That's just an expectation in the marketplace. We have those same discussions every year with every supplier."

Gia spoke up. "I think another is responsiveness. I think our customers would value a supplier who can be responsive to their needs. You know, within reason."

Jeremy nodded in agreement. "I could see being more responsive on volumes and on new product designs. You know, with producing trial parts and so forth. Let's keep those points in mind as we work on our vision."

Next, Jeremy had them pair up. Each pair would have ten minutes to come up with a draft vision statement. They'd review each draft as a group and circle what they liked. Then, they'd pair up again and do more drafts.

Anya looked at him curiously and asked him, "Where'd you get this process from?"

"From my last bubble gum wrapper," he replied after scrambling for an explanation. He needed to say something. For a moment, he felt just a little guilty about telling a little white lie because the process was Josephine's, but he felt it wasn't the right time to tell them about his mentor.

"We'll see about that," she replied with a smile.

The pairs split up and worked on their vision statements. After the first round, the team was circling phrases such as "competitive advantage," "highest quality," "responsive production capability," "low cost," and "the partner of choice."

The second round of pairing found the team aligning to a very similar vision statement. Jeremy wrote all three on the flip chart. With some minor changes in wording, the team agreed on the following vision: "All Pro Manufacturing is the company of choice for leading equipment manufacturers because we provide our customers with a competitive advantage with high-quality, low-cost parts and a responsive manufacturing system." As Jeremy wrote the final version on a separate flip chart, he announced they'd take a ten-minute break so everyone could think about the vision.

As they reconvened after the break, Jeremy asked if they had any concerns about the vision statement.

Anya said, "I like it."

"Me too," said Charlie. The others nodded in agreement.

Jeremy said, "Okay." Then looking around, he asked, "Is this vision motivating? Is this what we're going after?" And then he paused. Again, there were looks of satisfaction on everyone's faces. Except for Gia.

Jeremy said, "Gia, you don't look convinced. Is there something missing or wrong?"

Staring at the flip chart, Gia said, "I want the word 'the' capitalized." Seeing confusion, she added, "So, it'd read 'All Pro is THE company of choice.' I want to be on top."

That seemed to resonate with others. "Me too," Bradley said. "I want us to be the top dog again. Like when I first started."

This time, there was energy and enthusiasm. Jeremy thought, this team wants to win. Looking around the table with a big grin, he said, "I like it. Congratulations! We have our vision, and it's only 3:30."

Anya laughed and said, "And all from a chewing gum wrapper."

Jeremy smiled and said, "Not quite. But we need to keep our mission and vision front and center. I'll send this out, and we'll post them in our office areas. I'd like you to review both with your teams. Let's take a short break, and then we'll start discussing how we're going to hit our new goals for the year."

With that, everyone but Jeremy left the room to take a stretch break. He moved another flip chart into place at the head of the table. It contained their goals for the rest of the year, including the two "impossible" Symmetry goals. Remembering Josephine's advice, Jeremy made a mental note never to use that phrase again, even just to himself.

Everyone was back in the conference room shortly before four. Jeremy told them they'd finish the day's work by five. He said he wanted to use their time until five to set the stage and framework for their strategy and goal session the next day, Friday.

He started by uncovering the flip chart, which had a bulleted list of goals for the rest of the year. The goals addressed cost of sales, overhead spending, and production growth. Those hadn't changed from the first of the year. It also included the two new goals for on-time delivery and quality. Those were written in red.

Pointing to the two red goals, he said, "First, I have to acknowledge these goals are very aggressive. We've talked about that." Everyone around the table nodded in agreement. He stepped back to look at both the vision and the goals at the same time and said, "If we focus on these goals, I think we'll be on the road to achieving our vision. To be THE supplier of choice." He paused and then said, "For all our customers, not just Symmetry."

Seeing a few frowns, he said, "I see concerns from some of you. Bradley, what are you thinking?"

Bradley, looking at the goals, said, "I don't see how we can hit all of those by the end of Q4. We're already in Q2. It would take a miracle."

Nodding, Jeremy acknowledged his concerns. He said, "I agree these are tough. But we made our Symmetry shipment, and no one thought we could. Thoughts?"

Immediately, Anya spoke up, "It would be great to be THE supplier of choice in our industry."

Others nodded in agreement. Jeremy was going to jump in, but Bradley beat him to it. "As long as everyone's signing up for what it's going to take." His gaze was fixed on Anya.

Jeremy saw Anya tense up. She said, "It looks like you don't think I can do it."

Bradley responded, "This is going to take a lot of work with our suppliers."

"I know that, and I'm willing to do the work," she said defiantly.

"Great," Bradley said. His look softened, "And I'm willing to help in any area, including suppliers, if you want my help."

"Okay. Thanks. I appreciate your offer," Anya said, her expression relaxed.

Unexpectedly, Aaron asked, "Are we really that far off on our goals?"

Jeremy turned toward Gia and asked, "What did you find when you looked at our shipments in Q1?"

Gia replied, "This last quarter, I noticed that a third of our late shipments were on new parts or parts where the customer had made last-minute changes."

Jeremy said, "That's good information. We need to keep that in mind because those situations continually come up. We get new parts or customer order changes all the time. What about quality? Do you have any quality information from Q1?"

Gia replied, "Only on Symmetry shipments. They're our only customer that gives us real-time information. Their shipments were at 91 percent."

Charlie chimed in. "Our quality rate was higher for Symmetry because we did 100 percent inspection on their replacement shipment and their other shipments after that."

"So, our quality levels for our other customers were lower?" Jeremy asked.

With a disappointed look, Charlie said, "Yes."

"Symmetry is our biggest customer, but we can't have lower goals for other customers. I'm assuming everyone would agree with that?" Jeremy asked, looking around the table.

"Definitely," Bradley said. "I just don't know how we get from 88 percent for Q1 to 99 percent by the end of Q4. For all of our customers."

Everyone nodded in agreement.

"That's what we'll discuss later, but I agree. It's going to be very tough," Jeremy said, looking at the goals on the flip chart.

Glancing at his watch, he said, "It's almost five. This is a good place to stop for the day. Tomorrow, we'll jump into strategies to reach our goals. We're having dinner on the patio by the lake at 6:30, and I hope you can all make it. Thanks, everyone, for a productive afternoon."

With that, everyone packed up and headed out of the conference room. Jeremy saw Anya and Bradley talking in earnest as they left. It looked like they had developed a stronger relationship. He'd need that over the next three quarters.

Generating Breakthrough Strategies

The group was back in the conference room at Grand Lakes promptly at eight Friday morning. Dinner the night before had been a wonderful, relaxed event, and everyone seemed more at ease this morning.

Jeremy started the morning by doing a quick recap from Thursday. Then, he reviewed their team mission, vision, and rules before starting the next section. He reminded them they'd do that before every meeting.

"I know this is the part we've all been wanting to get to. We need specific strategies to achieve our vision and tough goals, and this morning we're going to come up with those strategies. Then, this afternoon, we'll develop our individual goals to make sure we deliver our strategies and hit our team goals. It's going to be a busy day, but we should walk out with our game plan for the rest of the year. Ready?"

Everyone nodded yes. He continued, "To make sure we generate ideas for different strategies, we're going to divide into two groups. Each group will brainstorm ideas to improve both our quality and our on-time delivery goals. One group will stay in the conference room, and the other will go down to the lounge area. We'll reconvene in forty minutes. In the end, our goal is to have at least five but no more than seven strategies we will focus on. Any questions?"

He put Aaron, Charlie, and Anya in one group, and Jeremy joined Bradley and Gia.

Being the organized group, Jeremy's team got right down to business. They divided the forty minutes into two segments for the two goals. They tackled on-time delivery first. Jeremy started by saying, "Bradley, I know you have ideas."

Bradley had brought the proposals he'd told Jeremy about. He identified four stations on the production line that were bottlenecks to higher throughput and also had reliability issues. He said replacing them would improve quality, throughput, and responsiveness.

Jeremy said, "Great. Let's put that at the top of the list."

"Don't you want to know how much that's going to cost?" Bradley asked.

"No, we're brainstorming right now, and I want to get ideas on the table. We'll discuss cost later. I have one. Because we're having issues with new parts, we could connect with engineering before they finalize their designs for customers," Jeremy said.

Bradley said, "We've tried, but they haven't been willing to include us."

Jeremy smiled. "Remember, I used to work in engineering, so hopefully I have an in."

Gia jumped in next. "Based on what we saw on late shipments, I'd like to see if we can get information about changes in customer orders earlier. Then we could be ready for them."

Jeremy smiled. "Good idea. We'll have to see how we can get that information. Sales must get wind of those changes before anyone else, but we'll have to check. I'll add it to the list," Jeremy said.

They talked through other ideas. By the time they were done, they had five solid suggestions for both quality and on-time delivery.

The energy level was high as everyone reconvened in the conference room. Between the two groups, they had thirteen strategies. Using a team voting process, they selected six strategies: upgrade the production line, install a new process control management system, improve supplier quality, partner with engineering on new part manufacturability, customer order coordination with sales, and a responsive inventory stocking strategy. The six strategies were posted on one flip chart at the head of the table.

Jeremy stepped back and surveyed the team. "Are these six the most important areas we can focus on to hit our goals?" he asked. The high energy that had carried them through to this point was fading. He had them take a break.

When he came back, he saw several of his staff standing in front of the strategy list.

Without any prompting, Bradley said, "This is going to be a lot of work."

Others nodded in agreement. Charlie said, "And we're going to have to stay tied at the hip."

Hearing their concerns, Jeremy asked, "Is this too much? Do we need to cut anything back?"

Gia spoke up, "It's a lot. But I'm really excited by the results we could achieve." Then she said, "It will be challenging to keep everything on track."

Others voiced their agreement. Jeremy said, "That's why I'm going to ask each of you to take a strategy and make sure we stay on track. And we're all responsible. I'm not abdicating final responsibility, but doing all this will require everybody on board."

Gia looked excited and said, "I like the idea." Others nodded in agreement.

He said, "Let's get started." Then he walked to a blank flip chart. He wrote "Process Control System Implementation" at the top of a flip chart sheet. Turning to the group, he said, "For each strategy, I want to come up with major milestones, key players, potential roadblocks, costs, and owner. Every strategy will have an owner."

Turning back to the flip chart, he wrote "Milestones" below "Process Control System." They briefly discussed the new software and equipment that would be required. He then had the group discuss the possible milestones and timeline for implementing the system. It started with deciding which system to buy. Charlie thought he'd have that done within two weeks because he'd already been looking at different options. Then they outlined the other big milestones. Key players included Ken, the manufacturing staff, engineering, and suppliers. They had an energetic discussion of the roadblocks once they agreed on the scope of the initiative. Resistance from suppliers was identified as one of the biggest roadblocks, and they briefly discussed how to address it.

Jeremy asked Charlie for a ballpark figure for the cost. He replied it would probably cost $300,000, assuming they bought a basic system without the advanced reporting options. The owner of the strategy would be Charlie.

They did the same for the other five strategies so that there was a single owner for every strategy per the list on the flip chart.

- Charlie   Process Control System Implementation
- Bradley   Production Line Upgrade
- Jeremy   Engineering Engagement
- Anya   Supplier Quality Initiative
- Gia   Inventory Management Initiative
- Aaron   Sales Coordination Initiative

Jeremy asked Aaron to set up a master Excel file to track the major milestones for every strategy. The review highlighted how the six strategies were intertwined. The quality system implementation, for example, would have a significant impact on the supplier and production line strategies. They adjusted milestone dates based on that discussion.

It was almost noon by the time they finished the discussion of all six strategies. Jeremy said he'd post the strategies around the conference room so they could review them in the afternoon when they'd discuss their SMART goals. Anya asked, "What are SMART goals?"

Jeremy could see the group needed lunch, so he said, "Good question. We'll discuss that after lunch." As they headed out the door to the patio below where lunch was set up, Jeremy thought about how exciting the morning had been. He felt better now that they had strategies, but he now understood how much work it was going to be.

Lunch on the patio was a welcome break from the morning's intense discussion. Jeremy noticed that the discussions taking place were open and personal, not about All Pro or their looming goals. Bradley and Gia were trying to get tickets for a professional lacrosse game. Charlie, Aaron, and Anya were debating private versus public universities. He thought back to the start of Q1, less than four months ago. Those discussions would never have happened. And they wouldn't have been going back to a conference room with great strategies posted on the walls. Now, they needed to integrate the strategies with their individual goals for the rest of the year so they'd stick.

Building Personal Accountability for Strategies and Goals

The team members slowly walked back to the conference room, continuing their personal discussions. Jeremy did a quick check-in to see if anyone had any questions or concerns. No one did, and everyone looked ready to move on. Not surprising, as it was Friday afternoon.

He said, "I want to get us out of here by 4:30 this afternoon. But I want to make sure each of us knows what we need to do over the rest of the year to keep the business going while implementing the strategies we developed this morning. We're all going to have a lot going on, so we're going to each work for about an hour to develop our SMART goals for the rest of the year. For those of you who aren't familiar, SMART goals are specific, measurable, attainable, realistic, and time based. Our goals should all be SMART."

Anya said, "Do you have an example of one?"

Jeremy said, "Good question, because SMART goals are challenging to write. One of mine will be to develop a metrics package and business review cycle by Monday that will keep our team on track to implement our six strategies. What I'm going to do is specific and measurable. It's time bound because I have a deadline of Monday, and it's attainable and realistic."

Anya was taking notes and said, "Thanks."

He'd written the SMART definition on a flip chart sheet and posted it on the wall.

Bradley said, "You want us to combine our ongoing responsibilities and our strategy work into our own individual goals quarter by quarter. That makes sense. We can see if it's all doable."

"Exactly. Here are some sheets you can use to document your SMART goals for each quarter," Jeremy said as he handed out sheets of paper. "We'll review in an hour to make sure we're on the same page."

With that, everyone found a place to work. Most stayed in the conference room so they could see the notes that had been posted on flip chart paper around the room.

At the end of an hour, they reconvened and walked through their SMART goals. Anya and Aaron's plans were modified the most. After Aaron finished reviewing his SMART goals with all the modifications, he said, "Thanks, I have a better understanding of how things work here."

Anya's SMART goals were modified because she didn't realize how quickly her suppliers would need to change their processes and results.

When she reviewed her SMART goal on implementing process control modules at suppliers, Charlie said, "You'll need to move the implementation up a month to sync up with our internal system testing."

She said, "My team doesn't have the bandwidth to support that time frame, and a lot of our suppliers aren't going to support it with staffing either."

Charlie said, "I'll see if our team can help on that."

That was just one of several changes in her SMART goals. Jeremy could see disappointment on her face. He needed to check in with her to see how he or others could help.

The review of goals was finished at 4:30.

Jeremy said, "We got a lot done today. Thank you for all the hard work. I'll send copies of everything by Monday morning. FYI, I do expect your individual list of goals to be a living document that I'll review with you at our regular one-on-one meetings. And, as a team, we'll discuss next steps at Tuesday's staff. I want every strategy owner to manage the overall strategy and raise a flag when we're off track. Any questions before we go?"

There weren't any, but Jeremy couldn't tell if that was because no one had any questions or if his staff was just eager to go home.

As everyone started packing up their things, he said, "Have a good and relaxing weekend."

Jeremy caught Anya as she was leaving and asked, "Are you doing okay? I know there's a lot riding on your management of our suppliers. They're key to our success."

Nodding in agreement, she said, "I'm really glad we had this session. It's been a great education. I just don't want to let this team down. I'm going to work on my plan some more over the weekend. I really need that third buyer."

Jeremy said, "I agree. I just got an approval from Ken to make that hire. I'll forward it to you. Let's follow up Monday morning. Have a good weekend with Noah."

She smiled and said, "Excellent. That's a relief."

With that, they got in their cars to leave. Before he pulled out of the parking lot, Jeremy sent a text to Josephine asking if she could meet Saturday or Sunday morning. While he felt satisfied with the results from the offsite, he needed ideas on keeping the team on track. He knew it would be a long haul to hit their Q4 goals. Then he headed home.

STEP 4

Deliver Results

Sunday, April 23

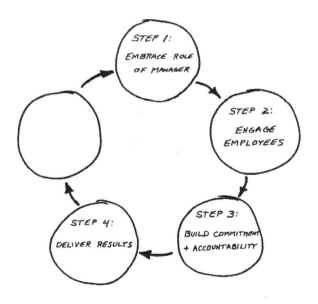

Keeping the Team on the Track to Success

Josephine met Jeremy at Roast bright and early Sunday morning. She wanted to meet at seven because she was going paddleboarding with her husband at nine at Avila Beach, just ten miles from San Luis

Obispo. Once they were seated with their coffee and a blueberry muffin, she asked, "How are things going on your *impossible* goals?" She emphasized the word "impossible."

He laughed. "You were so right to reframe the goals. When I changed my mindset, it changed the goals into something to aspire to." Then he filled her in on the team's progress at the offsite.

"Wow, I'm impressed you were able to pull that off in such a short period of time. Do you think the team is engaged in the business?"

He said, "They're definitely engaged. Now, we need to execute our strategies and manage the business to achieve our goals." He wished he felt completely confident in knowing they'd be successful.

She must have seen his self-doubt. "That's what step 4, 'Deliver Results,' is all about. You need to manage the performance of your team to achieve your goals."

"Your companies were famous for their achievements. From what I understand, you often beat the odds. How'd you manage that?" he asked.

She sat back, looking at the window as if she were recalling those achievements. Then she said, "There are a couple of keys I can share. First, you have to have usable metrics to understand if you're making progress toward your goals."

Jeremy was taking notes. He looked up at her and said, "Our year-end metrics are defined for us already."

She smiled and said, "That's good. You need to break them down into quarterly metrics so you can see if you're on track. Make the metrics visible not just to your staff but all of manufacturing. Some of your functions, such as purchasing and production, may need their own metrics to stay on track." She asked then, "Have you heard the saying 'What gets measured gets done'?"

"Yes, I've heard it and seen it in action. It's true."

"Second, you and your team have to be diligent about reviewing those metrics and your progress so you can make sure you're on track."

"I noticed you emphasized 'your team.' I intend to keep them involved," he said.

"Good. They need to feel as much ownership as you do. For all the goals. This is when a lot of teams get sloppy. They start out strong in reviewing results and actuals against their plan, but they don't reinforce that the whole team is responsible. With some of my teams, when we had tough goals, I used a team scorecard. Kind of like a baseball scorecard."

He jotted that down. "I like that. And then, my plan is to use my weekly staff meeting to keep us on track. I've got an agenda that'll work. At least I think it will. And I think Aaron could put together a scorecard."

"Good. That leads to the third thing you need to do." She paused then.

"Which is?"

"You have to hold yourself, your employees, and the whole team accountable. That means feedback. Lots of feedback."

"That's not my favorite thing to do, but I feel like I'm getting better at it," he said.

"That's really good, Jeremy, but you have a long haul ahead of you. It's going to be really important to keep the team positively motivated. When results are good and plans are being executed on time, make sure you give lots of positive feedback. You almost need to become a cheerleader."

"A cheerleader? I'm not the cheerleader type, in case you haven't noticed," he said.

She laughed. "I have noticed. But your employees and the whole team will thrive on feedback, especially positive feedback that's immediate. Look for what people are doing that's good, and then let them know right then and there. Shoot for a ratio of making three to five positive remarks for every negative remark. Your team will thrive on the positivity you create."

"Positivity? Is that a word?"

"It is. Look it up. Did you know people and groups can use more of their thinking brain when they're feeling good? That's when you'll get more ideas and more positive interactions from your team. And you'll have more fun."

He said, "I think I know what you mean. I've seen that." He added "positivity on team" to his notes. "I'm going to have to work on that ratio. Maybe I could add it to my to-do list."

"That's a good idea. You did that with leaning into situations, and it worked," she said. "You'll still need to give negative feedback on performance on occasion, but you've already been doing that when you see behavior that's not good for the team. Use that same approach. Do it immediately, be specific, give them a chance to explain, confirm they'll change future performance, and, most importantly, make sure they feel valued."

He was furiously scribbling notes. "Okay," he said.

She glanced at her watch. "I have to go. We have to get on the water before it gets too windy."

With that, he headed home.

On Sunday night, Jeremy planned his week. If the team was successful in the upcoming week, it would set the tone for the rest of the year. He organized his deliverables and key meetings using Excel and Outlook. His priorities this week included setting top-level metrics for the team by quarter, outlining the review process for ensuring they met their goals, managing the six strategies, and continuing to run the business of shipping products to customers. They were all intertwined, of course, which would make it more challenging. He needed to ensure there was clear accountability. Finally, he sent his staff an email to let them know Tuesday's weekly staff meeting would be three hours long. They'd need that much time to get through his agenda.

The Same Old Monday Morning

When Jeremy walked in to work Monday morning, the warm and fuzzy feeling he had had Sunday night evaporated as soon as he stopped by the production line to see how things were going. The line was down. Production had stopped. *Yikes*, he thought. He assumed the line should be going full blast given the shipments they had to make this week.

When he asked where Bradley was, one of the production employees directed him to the conference room just down the hall.

When he walked up to the door, he could see Charlie and Bradley having what appeared to be an angry discussion. Bradley was talking vehemently at Charlie, who sat with his arms crossed and a deep frown on his face. Jeremy said, "I see the line is down. What's going on?"

They looked at each other. Neither appeared to want to say anything. Finally, Bradley broke the silence. "On Friday, we produced three hours of bad parts because our process control equipment wasn't calibrated correctly. Now we're behind on shipments this week, and we're going to have a lot of scrap materials because we can't fix the parts."

Charlie responded quickly. "Your team should have seen the equipment wasn't within specification. They're supposed to check it every thirty minutes. They let it go too long. Don't you train your production employees?" It sounded more like an accusation than a question.

Bradley immediately countered, "Your team was supposed to make sure the equipment was set up correctly in the first place. It wasn't. Even the parts that were produced right after your team calibrated the equipment were bad. We can't ship them."

As Jeremy listened to the exchange between Charlie and Bradley, he realized he was even more disappointed by the angry and attacking discussion going on than by the line being down. Choosing his words carefully, he said, "It looks like the rules we came up with at the offsite went out the window." He paused. "I believe the two of you can resolve this issue, but a positive approach focused on problem solving would be more appropriate."

Shaking his head, Bradley said, "You're probably right, but this is really bad. To make up for this, my team's going to have to put in a lot of overtime this week. And they did so much of it in Q1, they're burning out."

Looking at Bradley, Charlie said, "My team's affected too. It's not just your team all the time. My team has to support the line." He paused. "Sometimes I think you forget about the other teams."

Bradley was just about to respond, and Jeremy could see it wouldn't be productive, so he stepped in. "Okay. I see you're protecting your employees. But you also need to keep in mind that you're on the leadership team and how you work together is critical for the company and your employees. I'd recommend you focus on problem solving. Also, let me know ASAP if you aren't going to be able to make shipments this week. I'll need to let Ken know. I need to go."

With that, Jeremy walked out. He thought about his response to the discussion between Bradley and Charlie and wondered if he should have handled it differently. He made a note to talk to each of them individually. Sighing, he headed to his office.

Establishing a Framework with Metrics and Reviews

By the time Tuesday afternoon's staff meeting arrived, Jeremy felt like he'd already had a full week. From the looks of his staff members, they must have been feeling the same way. He started the meeting by saying, "It has already been a crazy week, and it's only Tuesday." He saw nods of agreement from several of his staff. Continuing, he said, "Thank you for working through some difficult situations. We'll talk about where we are on this week's shipments later in the meeting."

He paused and, looking around, said, "Before I go through the agenda, I want to remind all of us of our mission, vision, and team rules. These are what I see as our team framework. They are so critical that I'm going to read them at the beginning of every staff meeting." He continued, "Our mission is to produce state-of-the-art electro-mechanical parts for automotive, medical, military, and high-tech equipment manufacturers. All Pro Manufacturing is THE company of choice for leading equipment manufacturers because we provide our customers with a competitive advantage with high-quality, low-cost parts and a responsive manufacturing system."

Then he read the six team rules. He looked around the table and said, "Every one of us has to try to live these rules. It'll be easy when things are going well but a lot harder when problems come up. The first rule, assuming good intentions, is going to be especially important because we can't afford to have finger pointing and blaming."

Anya, Gia, and Aaron had questioning looks on their faces. They knew there was a problem with the line but didn't know about the argument between Bradley and Charlie. Bradley was nodding in agreement, and Charlie was making a note on his notepad. It was a good reminder for all of them.

Jeremy moved on. "I know we've got a lot on our plates with keeping the business going while making huge strides. Especially in quality and on-time delivery. I read somewhere that trying to make big improvements like we're doing is like rebuilding a plane while flying it."

"That's a good analogy. We don't want to crash," said Anya.

Jeremy smiled at her comment. "Yes, no crashes. I'm counting on our mission, vision, and team rules to help keep us on track. Now, let's talk about our agenda." He walked to the flip chart and, picking up a pen, began writing. "We have three agenda items: metrics/sub-metrics, strategy execution, and ongoing business. That's what we're going to discuss today, and this is what our general agenda will look like for every weekly staff meeting in the near future. Metrics will help us know if we are making progress. Reviewing our execution plan will help keep us on track with our strategies. And then we'll discuss ongoing business, like the line down situation we had yesterday, to make sure the plane's still flying."

He looked around to see if there were any questions. He didn't see any, so he said, "Let's discuss metrics."

Looking intently at the team, he said, "We need to ensure we stay on track to be successful. That's where metrics come in. What are the *team* metrics we should track to know if we are being successful?" He'd emphasized the word "team."

Gia interrupted by asking, "Can I ask a question?"

He nodded and said, "You bet."

"I noticed you emphasized the word 'team.' Was that on purpose?"

"I'm glad you asked. It was intentional. It's those measures that are so critical that the whole team is accountable for all of them. If we don't deliver on those metrics, then none of us succeeds. And vice versa."

Gia said, "Don't we already have those? Aren't those the quality and on-time delivery goals that Symmetry gave us? Aren't those our metrics? The 99 percent quality and 98 percent on-time delivery?"

Jeremy nodded. "Yes, those are two of the metrics we need to track."

Frowning, Charlie said, "We won't get there immediately. That 99 percent should be our Q4 goal."

"Exactly," Jeremy said. Then he said, "We'll create quarterly goals to get to 99 percent." He wrote "Q1," "Q2," "Q3," and "Q4" as bullets on the flip chart under quality and wrote "99 percent" next to Q4. "What should we shoot for by the end of Q2?"

Charlie said, "We were at 88 percent for actual quality at the end of Q1." Jeremy wrote that under Q1.

"If we evenly space the improvements out, we'd be at 92 percent by the end of Q2 and 96 percent at the end of Q3," Gia said.

Charlie and Bradley immediately reacted with looks of consternation. Charlie said, "We'll just be implementing the new process control management system at the end of Q2."

Bradley nodded. "And we won't have the new production stations in operation until the first of Q3. There's a good chance our quality goes down before it goes up."

Gia said, "If we don't, there'd have to be huge leaps in Q3 and again in Q4 to hit our numbers by the end of Q4."

Bradley and Charlie looked at each other. Charlie said, "Yes, and we'll see improvements. I'm just not sure how much. I'm modeling those right now. I'll know more after we meet with the software vendor on Thursday."

"That will be good to get. Let's put placeholders in for now. We'll say our quality goal is 92 percent for Q2, 95 percent for Q3, and 99 percent for Q4."

"Okay," Charlie said without a lot of enthusiasm. Jeremy saw that and said, "Let us know what your models show, okay?" He didn't want to leave Charlie believing he couldn't raise concerns. Jeremy asked Charlie to set up a meeting with him on Friday morning to discuss what he learned from the vendor.

Jeremy said, "We have our first, top-level team metric by quarter. Now, what about sub-metrics for quality? What are the key areas that are going to drive that metric that we need to measure?"

Anya jumped in, saying, "Supplier quality. To produce good parts, we need good incoming materials."

Jeremy said, "Yes, that would be a sub-metric. We'll need our suppliers to at least match our goals by quarter. So, if our quality metric is 92 percent for Q2, our suppliers would need to be at 92 percent too." Everyone nodded except Anya as he wrote the rates in for the supplier quality sub-metric.

With a pensive look, Anya said, "We're reviewing contracts of key suppliers right now. We're going to need to change our terms, and they're going to charge us more. They'll need to improve their process control systems, and they'll have more scrap materials."

"Supplier quality is critical for our success," Jeremy said.

"I know," Anya said. Her response was unusually short. She was clearly worried about her suppliers' ability to hit those rates.

"What are the other sub-metrics that are going to drive our quality team goal?" Jeremy asked.

Bradley quickly said, "Production line quality. The quality of parts produced by our production line."

"I think everyone would agree. Is that one metric for you?" Jeremy asked.

"Overall? Yes. I may set metrics by station for my own purposes. You know I like detail," Bradley said with a smile.

"Good," Jeremy said. "Should your targets for each quarter be the same as the overall team metric by quarter? So, if the overall quality metric for Q2 is 92 percent, your end-of-the-line metric is 92 percent?" Jeremy asked.

Bradley simply said, "Yep."

So they had their second sub-metric under quality. When Jeremy asked if there were any other areas that would affect quality they should measure, no one could think of one.

Jeremy smiled and said, "We have our first metrics for the team." Looking around, he said, "So, every one of us is accountable for achieving our quarterly quality metric." He paused, looking at Charlie. "Charlie, because you're the quality manager, you'll be responsible for reporting our actuals against our target. And for giving us warning when you realize we're not going to hit it."

Charlie nodded in agreement.

Jeremy said, "The person who has the area measured by the sub-metric will be accountable for achieving that sub-metric. So, Anya will report on supplier quality. And Bradley will do the same for production line quality. Any questions?"

Charlie asked, "How often will we report the results?"

Glancing over at Aaron, Jeremy said, "We're going to put together a monthly scorecard with all our team metrics and sub-metrics. Aaron has experience with that, so he's working on the design now."

Aaron said, "I'm going to keep it simple and report targets and results for each metric. I'll use color-coding to show if we're not meeting, at risk of not meeting, or actually meeting the target. You know, like red, yellow, and green dots. That way, we'll be able to quickly focus on the problem areas."

"Thanks, Aaron. That sounds perfect," Jeremy said. "If you have an area that's red or yellow, you'll be able to investigate and report to the team. I want our team meetings to focus on actionable information. We'll try this approach and modify it as needed. Comments, questions?"

"This all sounds good," said Bradley. "We'll just have to see how it works. If we're not making progress and everything's red, that's going to be hard."

"I understand what you mean. But we'll know where we stand," said Anya. "My concern is how much time this is going to take to follow up. We already have a lot going on. I don't have a lot of resources."

"Me too," said Charlie. "My team is already lean, and then we're implementing the new process control system."

Jeremy looked around. Everyone was obviously concerned, and rightly so. He said, "This is a lot to do. We're going to need extra help. At least for the next six months. Can each of you get back to me by Friday if you need some extra temporary staff to get through the next six months? I'll go to Ken for additional overhead dollars."

Everyone nodded they would.

Jeremy said, "Good. Okay. We need to get back to other team metrics."

The metrics discussion continued. They identified four other team metrics, including on-time delivery to customers, cost of sales, overhead spending, and inventory. Every team metric had an owner, but the entire team was accountable for achieving the team metrics. Sub-metrics were identified for each team metric.

At the end of this discussion, Jeremy said, "We have our metrics, sub-metrics, and our team scorecard. Now, we'll review where we are on our six strategies."

Tracking Progress on Strategies

After taking a short break, the team took on the next agenda topic: status updates on the six strategies from the offsite. Jeremy listed the six strategies and their owners to remind everyone of their previous work:

- Charlie   Process Control System Implementation
- Bradley   Production Line Upgrade
- Jeremy   Engineering Engagement
- Anya   Supplier Quality Initiative
- Gia   Inventory Management Initiative
- Aaron   Sales Coordination Initiative

He asked Aaron to update the master strategy spreadsheet for each of the initiatives. Then, each owner reviewed his or her progress since the offsite. The process control system implementation and the production line upgrade were well on their way because Charlie and Bradley had already done quite a bit of work on them before Jeremy had started managing the group. They'd met that morning to coordinate key dates for implementation because elements of the process control system would be integrated into the production line upgrade. They'd also reviewed their presentations because they'd be discussing them with Ken and Jeremy on Friday. Assuming Ken was satisfied, he'd take the proposals to Richard, the CEO, for approval.

Jeremy asked, "What's the biggest issue you see with these two strategies?"

Immediately, Bradley said, "The cost. The line upgrade is going to be $2.8 million in capital spending and another $100,000 in overhead spending."

Jeremy said, "That's over the $2.5 million that Ken had said he was expecting. He'll want to know the details when we meet on Friday."

Charlie chimed in. "The new process control software itself is $200,000, and then there's an additional $200,000 to integrate it with our internal departments and key suppliers. Most of that's training on the system."

"Once we're up and running, the new line will save us labor and scrap because the line will be faster and less wasteful. Especially when the quality system is integrated," Bradley said. He looked at Charlie and added, "We'll include those savings for our presentation to you and Ken on Friday."

"Good work in such a short period of time," Jeremy said, nodding in appreciation. "I'm going to give Ken a heads up on the cost so he's not surprised on Friday. I know he doesn't want any surprises for Richard."

For his engineering engagement strategy, Jeremy reported that he'd scheduled a meeting with the engineering manager for the next Tuesday morning on how they could partner together more.

Next, Anya discussed the supplier quality initiative. "I'm having my buyers review every contract to understand what we require for quality and on-time delivery."

Jeremy asked, "So, we're not consistent on that?"

She quickly replied, "We have some contracts that are three years old, and some that are just one year old. We're changing the terms on those that are expiring."

"What about just holding suppliers accountable to meet the terms of their contracts?" Bradley asked.

Anya, sounding defensive, said, "We're trying to. We need to have our suppliers set up consistent process control systems to ensure that what they ship us meets our quality metric of 99 percent by the end of Q4. That's a lot of parts and suppliers to manage." She paused before saying to Bradley and Charlie, "I'm going to need your help on that."

They nodded that they would provide it.

Bradley said, "You should start with the most critical parts. There are probably twenty critical parts that cause 90 percent of our issues."

She said, "That list would really help. Even with adding a third buyer, we're thin on staffing."

Jeremy said, "We can easily add some temp labor, like I said."

Smiling, she said, "Good to know. Let me talk to my team to see how we could use them."

Gia and Aaron then discussed their strategies, inventory management and sales coordination. They were both on their way, with meetings set up in the next several days.

Jeremy asked Aaron to show the team his master strategy tracking spreadsheet. They reviewed the timelines for the major milestones for each of the strategies. They were on track to hit their first milestone of reviewing the process control system implementation and the production line upgrade with Ken on Friday.

Jeremy concluded the metrics and strategy review portions of the agenda by saying, "I know this was a long meeting, but we need to review our metrics and strategy implementation at every staff meeting to make sure we stay on track. So I'll continue to schedule three hours for every staff meeting."

Then he said, "Now, about flying the plane. Let's talk about this week's shipments."

The team hashed out the shipments that were at risk of not shipping on time over the next four weeks.

Gaining Support from Ken

Jeremy caught Ken in his office just as he was packing up his briefcase to leave for the day. Ken waved him in to have a seat. Jeremy filled Ken in on the outcomes from his staff offsite and meeting.

Ken said, "It sounds like you've got good strategies. Will you be able to deliver on Symmetry's goals?"

It was so like Ken to cut to the heart of the matter. Jeremy said, "We'll make significant headway, but I can't guarantee we'll hit those goals for Q4. We'll review two of the strategies on Friday with Charlie and Bradley. I wanted to give you a heads up. It looks like the total cost of those two strategies will cost about $3.2 million, which is more than we'd discussed before. We'll go through the details on Friday."

Ken frowned. "That's a lot more than I would expect, so you'd better have a good rationale. That's going to be a tough sell with Richard. I want to see what those upgrades are going to give us. I'm not sure he's going to buy the whole thing."

Jeremy countered, "I wasn't here when the line was originally installed, but Bradley said we haven't put any money into the line since then, except for repairs to keep it going. Most of the equipment on every station is way over the expected lifespan. It's just worn out. And the process control system is out of date and breaking down too. And it's not giving us the data we need to manage our quality."

Jeremy decided he might as well get all the impending financial news on the table and said, "We'll also need to hire some temp labor for about six months to get through the process control system implementation and the line upgrade and to get our suppliers in line. I'll also have those cost estimates for you on Friday."

Ken grimly said, "All right. We'll talk on Friday. Make sure you bring the data." Jeremy had been excused.

The rest of Jeremy's week was hectic, especially in preparing for the review with Ken on Friday. He'd told Charlie and Bradley to quantify their proposals as much as possible. He also asked Anya to provide information on suppliers, parts purchased, and the status of contracts so he could paint an accurate picture of their procurement situation.

On Friday, Jeremy started the review with Ken by discussing the metrics they'd established by quarter and the six strategies to achieve those metrics. Then, Charlie and Bradley did an excellent job of presenting their respective strategies. Ken asked questions throughout and kept pushing on lower-cost alternatives, but they were well prepared. He asked them to include several "what if" scenarios at different volumes of production.

Ken seemed satisfied with their presentations. At the conclusion of the meeting, Ken said he'd take the proposals to Richard on Monday morning for approval. He asked Jeremy to stay behind while Bradley and Charlie left the room. He said, "Jeremy, if Richard approves this spending, your team has to hit Symmetry's goals. I'm counting on you to deliver. For my sake as well as yours."

Jeremy swallowed hard. Trying to marshal his confidence, Jeremy said, "We'll do our best."

Things Get Worse Before They Get Better

Jeremy got the good news from Ken late Monday afternoon that Richard had approved all of their requests, with one caveat: they also had to add production capability to support 30 percent revenue growth next year. When Jeremy asked why, Ken said Richard thought they'd easily get that much additional business if Jeremy and his team achieved their goals this year. Jeremy thought, success breeds success . . . and more work. He told Charlie and Bradley. They were thrilled and immediately moved into action to place orders.

The structure Jeremy had implemented for the weekly three-hour staff meetings seemed to be working. At the start of every meeting,

Jeremy read the mission, vision, and team rules. No one raised objections about hearing them every week.

It worked better than Jeremy expected to have the metrics discussion first on the agenda of every meeting. It reinforced team accountability for the top-level metrics. With that accountability, the team members' discussion of their actual results versus their goals was open and animated. The team scorecard provided visual cues so the team could focus on the metrics that were yellow or red. Jeremy wanted to guarantee the team members didn't lose sight of their accomplishments, so he made sure they touched on the green metrics as well. That gave him the opportunity to give positive feedback. He noticed others were making positive comments as well. He hoped it was becoming contagious.

The second agenda item, reviewing their progress on the six strategies, was also yielding benefits. Their six strategies were intertwined, so the meetings provided a way to coordinate their activities. They were on track throughout Q2 on their strategies, but one thing became apparent very quickly: most of their strategy work in Q2 would have little positive impact on Q2's results.

One of the six strategies, the sales coordination initiative, was the exception. The sales department had quickly seen the advantage of giving manufacturing early warning on customer order changes. The sales staff members invited Aaron to attend their weekly sales update calls so he could hear about possible changes in orders before they became a reality. That gave Anya and Bradley extra time to adjust their purchase and production plans. Their on-time delivery metric had already improved one percentage point from Q1. To hit their Q2 goals would just require very hard work and some luck.

Their luck ran out the first week of June, when their quality results tanked. Charlie and his team were just beginning to implement the new process control system, while, in the same week, parts were being produced for a new customer for the first time. Charlie was in overload but hadn't requested any additional resources even when Jeremy had pointedly asked in one of their staff meetings if he needed them. Charlie's team failed to upload the quality specifications from the new customer, so Bradley and his team were using default specifications without knowing it. Almost 30 percent of the parts had already been produced before it was caught. The parts already produced had to be scrapped and replaced. They missed making their shipments on time. Manufacturing had been teetering on the edge of not making its Q2 metrics, and this pushed them over. They weren't going to make it.

Jeremy was frustrated when he heard about the missed shipments and the cause. He knew it was important to address the error with Charlie.

Jeremy asked Charlie to meet him in his office. He first confirmed that it was Charlie's error in not giving his team the new specifications. Then, he asked Charlie what had happened to cause it. Charlie's face was lined with worry and remorse. He said, "I just missed it. I was going too fast and overlooked it on my to-do list. I know I messed up our Q2 metrics, and I apologize."

Jeremy looked at him thoughtfully and said, "I understand how that can happen. I'd offered to get you an additional resource, but you'd said your team could handle everything. My one recommendation in the future is to really think through when you need help, especially when it's being offered. I know you're sensitive about hitting your overhead targets, but if that's what's holding you back, please talk to me. We can probably find savings in other areas."

Charlie said, "I know I can be—what's that saying?—penny wise and pound foolish. I will really try to step back and look at the bigger picture."

Jeremy continued, "I really value your contributions and having you on my staff. I know you'll be successful in leading us to success in hitting our quality metrics in Q3 and Q4."

Charlie's frown had been replaced by a smile. He said, "Thanks. I appreciate your faith in me."

Jeremy said, "Now, please look at the next three months and let me know if you and your team need some temp staffing help. We have a little buffer in our budget."

Charlie said, "I will."

Starting the Last Month in Q2

The mood of the team at their first staff meeting in June was mixed. Aaron handed out the team scorecard for April and May. The Q2 scorecard wouldn't change much because they were already in month three of the quarter.

Their performance had improved from Q1 because they were looking further ahead at shipments. Unfortunately, only one team-level goal, inventory, was green against their Q2 goal. They were red in all other metrics, including quality and on-time delivery. The team sat glumly looking at the results.

Gia asked, "Does Ken know about this? Us probably not hitting our Q2 goals?"

Looking around the table, Jeremy said, "No, not yet. I don't want to lose sight of our progress in our metrics from Q1. Our hard work is paying off."

He looked at the scorecard again. "But I know we're not going to hit our goals for the quarter. I want to find out where we are with our strategies and get your feedback on how those strategies are going to affect how we do in Q3 and Q4. I want to give him that insight on the future if possible."

They reviewed each of the team goals and the sub-goals below them. Jeremy started the review by saying, "We need to understand what happened so we can avoid the same mistakes or situations the rest of the year."

On-time delivery was the metric with the biggest gap in actual results versus the target. The actual rate was 87 percent versus their Q2 target of 92 percent, a five-point difference.

Looking around the table, Charlie said, "I really screwed up with that new customer specification. I apologize."

Jeremy said, "Thanks, Charlie, for bringing that up." Looking around the table, Jeremy asked, "Do we know what caused the other on-time delivery issues?"

Looking somber, Bradley said, "It was a mix of issues for production.

One of our biggest issues is high turnover on the stations we're staffing with temporary employees. It seems like, as soon as we get them trained, they leave for higher pay somewhere else. So, we spend time training instead of producing. It's affecting quality too. A lot of them are Millennials. They don't seem to care."

"Millennials? It's the fact that they're Millennials that's causing the issue?" Gia asked with a challenging tone.

"Well, most of them are Millennials. That's who's available," Bradley said.

Jeremy was going to jump in when Aaron beat him to it. "Maybe you're not selecting the right Millennials or candidates in general. I'm a Millennial, and I know lots of Millennials who'd love a good temp job. And they'd care about quality."

Gia said, "I'm probably a Millennial. I'm not sure of the cutoff, but I do quality work."

"Okay. I'm not bashing either of you," Bradley said. It looked like he was being ganged up on.

Jeremy jumped in. "How about if Aaron helps you with your hiring process for those positions? He could add that Millennial perspective that might help."

Bradley looked dubious, but he said, "As long as it doesn't slow us down on hiring."

Aaron said, "I'll keep that in mind. I'm looking forward to it." He was smiling. Bradley wasn't.

This will be interesting, Jeremy thought.

They reviewed each of the other team metrics and discussed the causes for the low performance. Jeremy took copious notes.

Next, they reviewed the master spreadsheet of the six strategies. They were on track to hit every milestone with the exception of the supplier quality initiative. Anya reported that, with her senior buyer on board, they'd been able to rewrite the contracts for the ten most critical parts. But they wouldn't finish all 110 parts that All Pro regularly used by mid-August. That milestone date was pushed out to mid-September.

The strategy that carried the most risk was the production line upgrade that would be fully installed on July 7, the second week of Q3. They would need to qualify the upgraded line over the weekend of July 8 and 9 to ensure it was operating as expected and that the parts produced met quality standards. If there were issues, the line could be down up to three weeks, the length of time required to bring in replacement equipment. That was an eternity for manufacturing and could have serious implications for All Pro's Q3 financial results. They needed a contingency plan.

Gia suggested she work with Bradley to see if they could build ahead on orders just in case. Everybody looked at Bradley. Jeremy asked, "What do you think of that idea?"

Bradley replied, "Good idea. That'd give us some breathing room, a buffer. We'd need to coordinate that with Anya and our suppliers too." Anya nodded in agreement.

Aaron added, "I can give sales a heads up so they can let us know of any big orders coming down the pike."

Jeremy beamed. "Excellent ideas. I really appreciate everyone jumping in."

After they'd reviewed the six strategies, Jeremy looked around the table and said, "We'll probably start Q3 in the red," waving the score-card around. "But we're on track to implement the six strategies. And I'm proud of this team for staying on task with rebuilding the plane. I need to fill Ken in, but I'd like to get a sense from this team on our chances for hitting our Q3 and Q4 goals. Do you think we can do it?"

There was a long pause, and Jeremy was beginning to get a hollow feeling in his stomach.

Bradley said, "I don't have a definite answer, but I think we're taking the right steps. I'm excited and a little nervous about what's going to happen."

"Me too," Charlie said.

The others were nodding their heads in agreement.

Jeremy summarized what he was going to share with Ken. His key points were that they'd improved their results from Q1 but had met just one of their Q2 goals. However, they had investigated issues and problems so they wouldn't be repeated. The team was on track to hit all their milestones for their six strategies, but it was too early to know if that would enable them to hit their Q3 and Q4 goals.

He asked if anyone had any suggestions or changes. Bradley reminded him that, with their line redesign, they'd be able grow production to support Richard's goal of 30 percent revenue growth for All Pro next year.

"Good add, Bradley," Jeremy said. He added that to his notes.

Jeremy stopped by Ken's desk on his way to his own and relayed that exact message. Ken frowned when Jeremy reported they would hit only one of their five metrics in Q2, but he was encouraged by their improvement from Q1 and their progress on the strategies. He added at the end, "With the money we're putting into manufacturing, we'd better see some significant improvements."

Jeremy knew when he was being dismissed, so he nodded in agreement and exited.

Finally, Progress Begins

It was the last Friday in July. The first month of Q3 was almost done. Jeremy was at his desk, finishing the last of his email messages. He couldn't remember ever being so busy. He and his team were keeping the plane flying with much of the plane under construction. He felt good about the progress manufacturing had made.

The weekly staff meetings were still working effectively, as were his regular one-on-one meetings with his staff. He held fast to them even when Gia and Bradley had each asked to cancel them because they were so busy. He'd rescheduled at their request but hadn't canceled any. Some were just fifteen or twenty minutes long instead of the usual hour, but they always proved worthwhile. He expected them to come in with at least one topic or concern. On his part, he always asked them how they were doing and what he could do to help them. He also made a point to walk by each of their desks once a day. Between the two approaches, he was able to give a lot of feedback, and almost all of it was positive.

Installation of the new process control management system within All Pro was complete, and the reporting from the system was as advertised. They were getting real-time quality control data from their internal material handling, production, and packaging stations instead of having to wait until finished parts exited the production line. They were able to catch problems earlier in the process. Integration of the new system with the existing ones at key suppliers by mid-August would yield earlier warning on supplier issues.

Using Jeremy's performance-based hiring process, Anya hired a senior buyer, Brian, who hit the ground running. Incoming part quality was already improving, especially for the most critical parts. Her team's challenge would be getting suppliers to increase their quality to the levels needed by the start of Q4.

Production had successfully built ahead on orders in late June and early July. The installation of the line on July 7 had been flawless except for one station that the vendor had repaired. Building ahead on orders saved them from missing shipments the week of July 10.

Aaron had worked with Bradley and his team to craft questions that would better predict performance by temporary employees. He'd also persuaded Bradley to implement a temp conversion process so that better-performing temps could move into regular employee positions after a six-month period. It was still early, but Bradley's quality of hires seemed to be improving.

For the inventory management strategy, Gia and her team had just finished modeling flexible inventory levels required to support more-responsive production. They'd be implementing that over the next month with the expectation that on-time delivery to customers would improve by at least one point.

Jeremy's strategy to work with engineering to improve part design for manufacturability was bearing fruit. He and Bradley were now sitting in on final part reviews with engineering before the parts were released for production.

The sales coordination initiative continued to pay off. Aaron was now a welcome member of the sales review team along with sales and marketing. Jeremy was beginning to worry that Aaron was becoming too valued on that team. Would they try to recruit him? He would need to have a next career move discussion with Aaron and probably Gia too. Their work with other departments in implementing the strategies was exposing their capabilities to other managers.

The transformation of the team was the most gratifying change that Jeremy saw. He thought about the state of the team after his ultimatum call with Ben at Symmetry Technology. It wasn't the same team. They were working long hours toward a common vision, and they were having fun. He was having fun. Sasha had told him that she'd never seen him happier when he came home from work.

He was looking forward to next Tuesday's staff meeting. The trend data had looked good, and Jeremy was hoping for a lot of green dots instead of the red they had seen in Q2. He anticipated their results would be better, but he had no idea of their newest sticky challenge.

July's Results and a Sticky Problem

It was 1:00 p.m., and everyone except Aaron was at the staff meeting in the manufacturing conference room. Jeremy said, "Aaron's going to be a few minutes late. He's printing our scorecard. Let's go ahead."

Jeremy read their mission, vision, and team norms as usual. He didn't know if it was his imagination, but the others seemed restless, pensive. He realized he wasn't totally focused on what he'd just read either. He asked, "Are you antsy about seeing our scorecard for July? I know I am."

That broke the ice. Anya said, "Definitely. I can't wait to see how we're doing."

Charlie was just about to speak when Aaron walked in. Aaron apologized for being late while he handed out the single-sheet scorecards.

There were a lot of green dots. And silence as everyone scrutinized the results.

Jeremy was the first to say anything. "These results look really good. I see three green dots, one yellow, and one red. Quality, on-time delivery, and cost of sales are green. Inventory is yellow, and overhead spending is red."

Looking at Gia, Jeremy asked, "Do you know what's driving our inventory to be yellow?"

Gia replied, "Yes, and I think it's actually good news. We're still ahead on orders from building ahead in June and July. And Bradley's been running the production line at full capacity to ensure it's working as expected."

Nodding his head in agreement, Bradley said, "Except for the one piece of equipment the vendor repaired when we were doing the installation, the line's been working really well. We haven't had any breakdowns."

"Good," Jeremy said. "I agree. The fact that it's yellow is good news. When will it be back to green?"

Gia said with confidence, "By the end of August. Well before the end of Q3."

Looking at Aaron, Jeremy asked, "What about overhead spending? I think I know the answer, but what's behind the numbers?"

He quickly replied, "Most of the $80,000 in overspending was due to the additional temporary staff we added starting July 1. We had some additional labor in the budget, but we added more than expected."

Jeremy shrugged and said, "I think I was the one who suggested more staff in several cases. Given the workload, I didn't want our plane to crash. I'll take overspending on temporary staff every time if we meet our quality and on-time delivery goals. If you still have tempo- rary staff, please review the current need and the timeline for reducing that staff if possible. I'd like to get our numbers down by the end of Q3." He paused to ensure everyone understood. "Any questions?"

There were none, so they reviewed the other metrics that were green: on-time delivery, quality, and cost of sales. They were within striking distance of their Q3 goals, and they were just one month into the quarter. It was likely that the strategies would yield additional improvements, especially with the work Anya's team was doing with suppliers and the fact that they were still figuring out how best to use the output from the new process control system.

They'd finished reviewing the scorecard and were just about to start discussing the status of the six strategies when there was a knock on the conference room door.

The first thought that came to Jeremy was whether there was an emergency. And yes, there was, for the whole team.

The knock on the door came from one of Bradley's leads in production. Bradley met him at the conference room door, and, after a quick conversation between the two of them, Bradley said, "We're having issues with parts on station number two. Key subcomponents aren't adhering to our component assemblies." He looked at Anya. "Have there been any changes to our adhesives?"

Surprised, Anya said, "No, we've been using the same adhesives from the same vendor since I started. Maybe it's something to do with the production line. Isn't station two one of the new stations?"

Jeremy saw they were jumping to conclusions. "This isn't the right time and place to discuss this. Charlie, Anya, and Bradley, can you get together and figure this out? Between the three of you, I know you'll get to the bottom of it."

They nodded in agreement and headed to production on the first floor.

It was just Jeremy, Aaron, and Gia left at the table. "That's not the way I expected to end the meeting. Do either of you have anything we should know about your strategies or this week's shipments?" Jeremy asked.

Neither Aaron nor Gia had anything, so they left early.

Jeremy stopped by Ken's desk to let him know about the adhesion issue. Then he checked email and voicemails before walking down to the production area. He wanted to see if they'd made any progress on the adhesion problem.

He heard raised voices before he got to the door. Looking in the window, he saw Bradley and Anya in an obvious argument. Bradley's arms were crossed, and he was scowling. Anya was leaning forward, saying something not to but at Bradley. He could see her hands were clenched tight. Charlie was leaning forward too, trying to interject something into the discussion.

Jeremy knocked at the door and then opened it. He said, "This discussion doesn't look or sound good. What's going on?" He looked at all three. There was a pause. Charlie said, "We're still talking about what's causing the adhesion problem. There could be several causes."

Anya quickly said, "Bradley's saying the adhesive is bad. It's the same adhesive we've been using."

Bradley said, "How do you know? When's the last time you talked to the vendor? Do you review their process control results? To verify they're testing the adhesive we buy from them? When's the last time you checked?"

"I don't know when it was last checked. Anyway, they'd tell us if they changed it," she snapped back. "What about your line? You have a new station. Has it crossed your mind that it could be the new station? You have to apply the exact amount of heat for the adhesive to work."

Bradley adamantly said, "We have sensors to tell us if the temperature is out of specification. They're showing that it's been at the right temperature. That's not the problem."

"Hold on. What are you doing to understand if it's the adhesive or the line or even something else that's causing it?" Jeremy asked.

Looking down, Anya said, "I've called the operations manager at the supplier. She's talking to the production and engineering manager now to understand if the adhesive formula was changed. I'm expecting a call back any minute. That should resolve the question." She checked her phone, sat back, and crossed her arms.

"What about their process control reports? Aren't you going to review those?" Bradley said.

She rolled her eyes and said, "My team's pulling those reports."

Charlie said, "If it'll help, one of my quality people can help look at those."

Anya said, "That will help."

"What about the production line?" Jeremy asked, looking at Bradley.

"I don't see how the line could be the problem. But I am having my team restart that station so we can measure the surface temperature," he said. "They'll just get the same temperature as the sensor."

"It's good to check, though," Jeremy said.

One of Bradley's employees knocked on the door. Bradley stepped out to talk to him. He came back a minute later with a guilty look. Sighing, he said, "The sensor was wrong. The heating surface was five degrees lower than it should've have been. The sensor must be defective."

He took a deep breath and then, looking at Anya, said, "I'm really sorry, Anya. I apologize. I hopped all over you, and it wasn't your adhesive."

Anya nodded and said, "Apology accepted and . . ." Just then, her phone rang. She looked at her phone and said, "Hold on, it's the supplier." She stepped out of the room for a few minutes. Coming back in, she didn't look pleased. "It turns out they changed the formula slightly. But that was two months ago. They didn't tell us because it was still in our acceptable range of performance."

Charlie said, "We should have re-qualified it for our use."

She shook her head and said, "I know. I can't believe they didn't tell us. I told them in no uncertain terms this can't happen again. They may lose our contract." Jeremy could tell she was angry. She looked at Bradley and said, "I shouldn't have been so adamant. It's just that you were like . . . accusing me of not doing my job. I apologize too."

"Let's talk about that later. What are you going to do now?" Jeremy asked.

Bradley said, "We've called the vendor to fix the sensor. We'll have to retest that module once it's fixed to make sure the whole module is working right. But, with a different adhesive, we'll need to make sure it works. We'll need the old formula back," he said, looking at Anya.

"That's exactly what I told them," Anya said.

Charlie said, "My team can help set up the testing to make sure we're testing the module, the adhesive, and the two in combination. Heat and adhesives can be tricky."

"That sounds like a good plan," Jeremy said. Then he looked at Charlie and asked, "Can you excuse us?"

Charlie mumbled, "You bet." He scrambled out the door with his laptop in hand.

Jeremy turned to look at Bradley and Anya, pausing for a moment to think about what he was going to say. "I used to see this pattern when I first started managing the group, but I haven't seen this in a while. I really value your ability to work well together, so I was surprised when I heard you arguing. It had gotten personal. And Anya, you rolled your eyes."

Shrugging his shoulders, Bradley said, "I think I own most of it. I should have stuck to the facts instead of jumping to conclusions right away. And I got personal when I talked about you doing your job."

Anya's face relaxed. Looking at Bradley, she said, "For my part, I shouldn't have reacted the way I did. And I definitely shouldn't have rolled my eyes. Sometimes, I don't realize I do it. I think I reacted so strongly because it's been so crazy." She paused and said, "I want to be successful, and I don't want to let the team down."

Nodding his head in agreement, Bradley said, "We all want the team to be successful, and we're all tired. I was just so disappointed because I thought, 'Holy crap, we're not going to hit our numbers.'"

Jeremy sighed. "We may not hit our numbers. We're making lots of changes and really pushing." He paused before continuing. "But I know we won't fail because of intent or lack of effort from the two of you, or anybody on the team. I know you can do great work together, so I hope the next time things get difficult, you'll take a deep breath and remember our team rules. I really value what you both do, individually and especially together."

They both nodded.

"Okay," he said. "Can you let me know what you find out tomorrow about the line repairs and the new formula for the adhesive? I'll have Aaron run some scenarios, but I think we can still hit our numbers in Q3 if the line is back up later this week."

Smiling, he added, "Who knows, that yellow dot we got for having too much inventory may be our best yellow dot ever."

That broke the tension. All three laughed. Jeremy walked out of the conference room and left Bradley and Anya coordinating plans for adhesive deliveries and line testing.

Reviewing Q3's Results

The manufacturing team reviewed Q3's final results at Tuesday's staff meeting. Jeremy wasn't sure how Q3 would turn out given that the adhesive situation hadn't been the only surprise.

Their scorecard had a lot of green for Q3. Every team metric was green except for overhead spending, which continued to run higher than plan. The good news was the overspending on overhead was offset by a lower-than-expected cost of sales. The new quality system and line upgrade were resulting in less scrap and rework than expected.

That was a point Jeremy made with Ken when they reviewed the Q3 scorecard. Ken accepted Jeremy's explanation and said he'd share that with Richard along with the progress manufacturing was making. As they were finishing their review, Ken told Jeremy that he was pleased with his results. Jeremy reminded him that it was the entire manufacturing team that had achieved Q3's goals. Ken said in his gruff voice, "Well, it takes leadership to make it happen." Looking at Jeremy intently, he said, "We're really counting on you to hit Symmetry's Q4 goals. We can't afford to lose their business. We'd have to make some big cuts in headcount. What do you need from me to make that happen?"

Jeremy thought about his question. "You went out on a limb by supporting our team's strategies. So, thanks for that. And we'll gain even more benefits from those strategies in Q4. I don't know if they'll be enough to get us to 99 percent quality and 98 percent on-time delivery. Those last two percentage points on quality are going to be very tough. My team's running some scenarios to see what needs to happen to get there. We don't have any clear solutions at this point. We also need to figure out how to sustain those rates. We can't just hit them one quarter and then let them drop off."

Ken nodded that he understood. "Well, let me know what you need. And again, Jeremy, good work."

Jeremy walked out in a fog. He should have been elated with Ken's remarks, but he kept thinking about not having any solutions to get those last points of improvement. He wanted to talk to Josephine again.

Josephine's Advice on the Home Stretch

It had been a month and a half since Jeremy had last met with Josephine. It was a more leisurely meeting because it was on a Saturday and Roast was relatively quiet at 8:00 a.m. She told him about her trip to Costa Rica to look at several new coffee farms and to play in the great Costa Rican outdoor playground. She was sporting a cast on her left wrist, which she'd broken while zip-lining through the jungle.

He filled her in on manufacturing's results in Q2 and Q3. She congratulated him on his team's results and asked, "Do you remember the doubts you had about being able to make significant improvements in a short period of time?"

"I do remember. We've grown a lot in terms of our manufacturing capabilities and as a team too. Thank you so much for your help."

He sat back then and said, "We hit our Q3 goals on all but overhead spending. But it's still going to be hard to get those last percentage points of improvement." And then he paused. "Have you been in that position before? Any recommendations?"

She had an intense look and first focused on him. Then she looked at the trees outside. "I have. That's the way business is in many respects.

It's going after what seems impossible, and it usually involves that last difficult stretch. You know, like running hard in that last mile of a marathon."

She smiled. "Except a marathon is a solo adventure. You have a whole team that's running hard right along beside you. Rely on your team just as you've been doing. You know they want to get to the finish line too. Take advantage of the power of your team."

Looking outside again, she said, "That's what worked for me. And it still works today."

Jeremy laughed. "That's a great reminder. I will."

"Good," Josephine said. "Now, how's Sasha doing?" she asked. They spent the rest of their time talking about personal plans for the rest of the year.

Getting to the Goal Line

Tuesday's staff meeting started as it normally did, with Jeremy reading the team's mission, vision, and team norms. By now, everyone felt they could recite them in their sleep. He said, "We've started our staff meeting this way for six months. Is it still valuable?"

Gia was the first to respond. "I think it is. It kind of grounds me. Helps me remember why I'm here." She must have thought she sounded uncertain because she quickly added, "Not that I don't know why I'm here. Of course, I get that."

Aaron laughed and said, "I know what you mean, Gia. It's so easy to get caught up in everything that's going on that hearing the mission, vision, and team rules brings it back to the basics."

"I didn't think I'd like hearing them every meeting, but it's my rabbit's foot," Bradley said.

"Rabbit's foot?" Anya asked.

"Yes, things have been working much better, so I want us to keep doing it," he said. "Otherwise, our luck may run out."

"That's interesting," Anya said. "I wouldn't want to change anything either." Grinning then, she said, "I can't believe they used to use actual rabbit's feet as a token of good luck. That's so gross."

Jeremy saw the discussion digressing into a debate on luck symbols, so he intervened. "Before we go too far off track, I can see we'll continue starting with our mission, vision, and rules."

"Now, for our discussion on metrics, I'd asked each of you to project how you think our metrics will turn out by the end of Q4 given our trajectory. Let's go through those."

The team went through every metric, with each owner presenting his or her estimate of the year-end result. The good news was that three of the five—inventory, overhead spending, and cost of sales—would be attainable based on their current trend line. The other two, quality and on-time delivery to customers, were more difficult to project. The trend line was encouraging, but the rate of improvement was leveling out. It wasn't clear that they'd hit their Q4 goals.

Jeremy said, "We all want to hit our goals and Symmetry's too." There were nods all around the table. He continued, "I'd like us to put our heads together again and see if there's more we can do to close the final gap. We're going back to what worked at our offsite and brainstorm with each other. So, let's break into two groups." He held his hand in front of him and drew a line down the middle of the table. "I'll work with Gia and Anya. Bradley, Aaron, and Charlie, you'll be in the other group. We'll take thirty minutes to see if we can come up with a couple of things we can do to further improve our results this quarter. Does everybody understand?"

Everyone nodded, and the two groups separated, with Bradley leading his group to the production conference room downstairs. Anya, Gia, and Jeremy stayed in the upstairs manufacturing conference room.

Anya started their discussion. "We're already in Q4. It's the third of October, and we're looking for solutions that'll generate results by the end of December. That's tight." Jeremy and Gia nodded their heads. She added, "We've already built better supplier quality from our suppliers into the trend line, but we're still short on meeting the quality goal."

She paused a moment and, looking at Jeremy and Gia, asked,

"What's working so far? It seems like we should look at what's worked as a starting point."

Gia said, "One definite pattern we're seeing is early information is really invaluable. Getting order information earlier from sales is really important. And working with engineering has helped make new parts easier to manufacture."

"That's a good point," Jeremy said. They mulled that over for a minute.

Anya suddenly looked up. Smiling, she said, "You know, Symmetry wants a supplier who'll meet their goals. We want to get to those same goals with Symmetry and our other customers. At least the big ones." She had an almost mischievous look on her face. Jeremy couldn't wait to hear what she was thinking.

"What if we demand more from our customers in order for them to get the benefits of our better results?" she asked.

Gia looked at her seriously. "Our better results are higher quality and better on-time delivery. That's what you're thinking."

"That's worth something to our customers, right?" Anya said.

Gia began to smile. "I think I get it."

Then it hit Jeremy. "I get it too," Jeremy said. "We're giving them more, so we can ask them for more. To give us earlier information. Is that what you're thinking?"

"Exactly!" Anya exclaimed.

Gia said, "I think you're on to something."

The other group members came back in. They were talking earnestly among themselves about data mining. Their quiet discussion was in contrast to the energetic discussion they had walked into.

"Wow," Aaron said. "This must be good."

Jeremy beamed. "We have something, but let's hear yours first."

Bradley, Aaron, and Charlie shared that the new process control management system was providing excellent data on how the entire manufacturing system and the different parts of the system were working. Charlie said, "It can also be used to predict performance." He'd emphasized the word "predict."

"What would that do for us?" Jeremy asked.

"We could put in all the variables for upcoming production runs and estimate the quality and on-time delivery results. Then we could run some 'what if' scenarios to see how we could improve those results," Bradley said.

"For example, we could see if having a supplier send certain parts earlier would improve our chances of on-time production," Aaron added.

"It's a module of the process control system I was going to delay implementing until next year, but we could install it this month," Charlie said. Then he added, "If Ken's willing to pay for it this year. It'd be $50,000. It'd help us close the gap for both on-time delivery and quality, but it'd probably put us over on overhead spending."

"That's a great option," Jeremy said. "We were planning to buy it next year anyway. I'll talk to Ken about it."

Then Gia, Anya, and Jeremy shared their group's idea of shifting their relationship with their largest customers from a supplier to a partner relationship. They'd ask those larger customers to share more information with them so All Pro could provide, in turn, higher-quality parts and improved on-time delivery. Gia made sure to tell them that it was Anya's idea.

Bradley looked at Anya and said, "That's a great idea if they'll do it. It'd make a huge difference to production." Aaron and Charlie nodded in agreement.

Aaron said, "It would make everyone's life easier."

Jeremy said, "That's a go then."

They then discussed what they'd ask their biggest customers, including Symmetry, to provide. The list included earlier information on orders, early involvement in new part designs, and a longer deadline on order changes. With those in place, the team estimated they could improve both quality and on-time delivery significantly.

Jeremy thanked the team for their ideas and said he'd talk to Ken about them. *What a team,* he thought as they left the meeting. We have two great options, and I didn't come up with either one.

He stopped by Ken's desk to discuss the two options. Ken's reaction was mixed. He wasn't happy about spending the $50,000 in Q4, but, when Jeremy outlined what they'd gain, he agreed to fund it. He said, "You've gotten great results so far. I love the data summaries that Charlie's sending out from the new process control system."

Jeremy knew there were advantages to having an analytical boss.

Then, Jeremy discussed Anya's proposal of asking All Pro's biggest customers to provide earlier access to information, including shipments and new part designs. Ken almost choked on the water he was drinking. "What? You want earlier information than they give now? I don't think they'll buy that."

Jeremy said, "We actually want to have them start thinking of us as a valued partner. A valued partner who can deliver better service to them if they reciprocate with better information. It's a different relationship. We should remember they want those improvements too."

Ken sat back in his chair. Glancing at his computer screen, he said, "I received an email the other day from Lee Smith, the chief operating officer at Symmetry. He was very complimentary of our Q3 performance. They're on track to launch products in the medical field, and our quality improvements are making a positive difference in their time to market. He might be open to your ideas. I'll give him a call."

It turned out Lee was very interested in All Pro continuing to improve its quality and on-time delivery. Symmetry agreed to meet All Pro's request for more lead time on orders and earlier involvement in part design. They pushed back on the deadline to make changes in orders but agreed to limit the magnitude of their changes. Symmetry would not change order quantities by more than ten percent up or down within two weeks of the delivery due date.

End-of-the-Year Results

It was finally the end of the year. Q4 had come down to the wire, but they'd met their Q4 goals. Jeremy had moved the staff meeting from Tuesday, December 19, to Friday, the 22nd. He wanted to have the final results on shipments. The last of the year's shipments had gone out late Thursday afternoon. Everyone was planning on taking Friday afternoon off because the company would be shut down the week between Christmas and New Year's, but they wanted to leave knowing the outcome for Q4.

Jeremy was five minutes late for the staff meeting because he was trying to stuff gifts into bags. His staff was seated when he walked in. Juggling the bags, he made his way to a seat at the table and sat down. Everyone was grinning ear to ear. He looked around confused. He expected everyone to be happy, but not grinning like it was a surprise party. Then he saw Bradley's shaved head.

He almost fell out of his chair. "You did it!" he exclaimed. "Wow!" Jeremy walked over to Bradley and tried to shake his hand.

Bradley engulfed him in a hug. "No, you did it. I am genuinely enjoying work. I didn't even mind shaving my head this morning. Actually, Alisha did it for me. She likes it. I might just keep it," he said, running his hand over his head.

Jeremy stepped back and said, "It does look good." He had calmed down by then, so he walked back to his seat and said, "Let's review our Q4 scorecard."

It was all green except for a yellow for overhead spending. The early purchase of the extra quality software module had put them over, so it was an approved yellow. The team members reviewed their metrics and the reasons for their success. Charlie was able to show that the predictive modeling enabled by the quality system software had gotten them the extra percentage point needed to meet their quality goal of 98 percent. Symmetry and two other big customers had started providing earlier order information, and their on-time delivery result was 100 percent. Not a single order had been late.

Jeremy summarized their performance by saying, "We've achieved the goals we thought impossible nine months ago. Congratulations." Everyone was beaming.

Bradley said, "I didn't think we'd get there. I think I remember saying that."

Anya grinned and said, "Yes, you did."

"Well, I guess I'll have to change my grumpy approach if we're going to be this successful," he replied.

"No, you don't. We need you to keep us grounded, so to speak," Gia said.

"I thought we could make it," Aaron said.

"You're young and optimistic," Charlie said with a smirk on his face. "You know, stuff happens."

"Yes, it does. And did," Gia added. "Remember our sticky problem?"

Jeremy saw Anya and Bradley exchange smiles. Anya said, "Slightly. That was painful."

The team digressed into talking about the different surprises and snafus they had encountered.

Jeremy didn't say much. He just listened, taking in the banter back and forth.

As it got close to eleven, he said, "I want to thank all of you for your hard work over the last year, especially the last nine months. I know it was a grind, but it was quite a ride, and I'm glad it was with each and every one of you." He was looking around the table.

He got nods and big smiles from all around the table.

"Finally, I know most of you are taking off for the holiday break. I hope you have a nice, relaxing time and enjoy your family and friends. I have a little gift for each of you." Then he handed out wrapped bottles of wine and plates of cookies he and Sasha had made the night before. He included a holiday card with a $200 gift card in each.

After shaking hands and giving hugs as everyone left the conference room, he went back to his office. Sitting on his desk was an envelope with a holiday card from Ken. He'd written, "Jeremy, congratulations on a great year. Go enjoy yourself next week." Inside was a $200 gift certificate to Bowen's, the best and most expensive restaurant in town. He made a quick trip to Ken's desk to thank him. He had a plate of cookies for him too.

Ken was meeting with Larry, his finance manager, when Jeremy stopped by. Jeremy knocked at Ken's door. His intent was just to drop off the cookies and then leave. Ken saw him through the glass and waved him in. Jeremy said, "Thanks for the card. I really appreciate it." He then handed Ken the cookies, noting that he and Sasha had made them last night.

Ken accepted them and said, "Good work this year, Jeremy." Larry was nodding in agreement. Then Ken said, "Richard and I would like to meet with you and your team to review your results. After the holidays of course." And then he turned back to Larry.

Jeremy hadn't anticipated this and said, "Sounds good." He'd said that nonchalantly, but he realized he didn't know if it really sounded "good." It sounded like more work.

Jeremy decided to put that out of his mind for the next week. He went back to his desk, packed up his backpack, and headed home to Sasha. He couldn't wait to start his long holiday week with her. He also wanted to connect with Josephine over the holiday break. He'd gotten through step 4 and was now beginning to think about his team and the need to renew before starting what would probably be another challenging year. Maybe she'd have some ideas on the review with Richard and Ken.

STEP 5

Renewal

Sunday, December 31

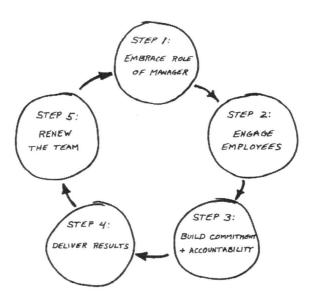

Josephine's Advice on Renewal

Jeremy met with Josephine on the morning of New Year's Eve. He told her he wanted to bring her up to date and discuss step 5, "Renewal." He was ready for this step. He also wanted to give her the present he and Sasha had selected.

He was waiting for her with his coffee on the table and the present in his backpack when she slid into the booth.

"Happy holidays, Jeremy. Are you enjoying your break?" she asked with a warm smile.

He beamed and said, "Definitely. We've had a great week. We even went to Monterey for an overnight stay and a fabulous dinner at one of Sasha's favorite restaurants. It's been great to get away and relax. How about you?"

"I'm enjoying the holidays too. I actually stayed in town and tried to get in here so my employees could spend more time with their families."

Then she said, "Don't keep me in suspense. I think I know, but how did everything turn out?"

"We hit our Q4 numbers! The team, as you said they would, came through with good ideas that helped us close that last gap. And the good news is the solutions are sustainable. They'll help us meet our numbers next year."

"That's wonderful news," Josephine said, beaming at Jeremy.

"Thanks, Josephine. Although Ken wants to do a review with Richard, himself, and our team after the first of the year. I'm not too worried. I think it's because we did pretty well."

She laughed, and he was a little taken aback. "Pretty well? You killed it." She must have seen him raise his eyebrows when she used that phrase. "My eighteen-year-old nephew's staying with us for the week, and he's rubbing off on me."

He laughed. "You sound like a . . . Millennial." They laughed together.

Then he asked, "Can we talk about step 5, 'Renewal'? When you first told me that was one of the steps, I thought it was fluff. You know, an optional step. But now, after these last nine months, I think I need to renew my team and myself."

She didn't immediately respond. "For me, step 5 is critical for my growth and even my mental state. And my team's too. We get so caught up in the day-to-day frenzy that we get exhausted, and also we fail to see how far we've come and how much we've grown."

Nodding, he said, "Yes, I think we're at that stage now. How do you suggest I do that?"

"Something I've done that works well is to have the team capture their story over the last period. For your team, it's probably the last year. I'd recommend telling your story on a big sheet of paper. You can see examples of storyboards or history maps on the Web. You do it as a group and really talk about what happened, who was involved, notable events and outcomes, and so forth. It's kind of like reliving the past, but with the goal of learning from it. What you want is to capture people's thoughts and emotions. And then you have the team step back and figure out what they've learned and what they want to make sure they carry forward."

Jeremy was writing notes. "That'd be a great exercise. I know I could fill in a lot with my thoughts during the year."

"Make sure you do. Even the negative ones. You'll build even more trust with your team," she said. "It's also a great way to recognize and celebrate everyone's accomplishments. Including the team as a whole. That's almost as important as learning from the map."

"That makes sense. I could have the team put the story together, and we can draw conclusions about the team. We could also each draw conclusions about ourselves. Individually," he said looking at his notes.

"Perfect," she said. "And this is where the five steps come full circle. You take that back to step 1, 'Embrace Your Role as a Manager.' You should do a self-assessment again because you're now a different manager, your business challenges are different, and your team is different."

"My employees should do that too," Jeremy said, adding that to his notes. She nodded her head in agreement.

He added, "This'll set me up to do their performance reviews. I haven't done them before, but I think they're due in February."

"Yes, and you can have them write their own," she said.

"Oh yeah. I bet they'll love that." He was thinking of his own experience in being on the receiving end of performance reviews.

"Actually, with the team story, it'll be a lot easier. And they should own their own performance and their growth, including future career decisions," she added. "Your job is to guide them and let them know if they're missing any blind spots."

He added that to his notes. Looking at Josephine, he asked, "Anything else I should know about step 5?"

"Nothing that I can think of. You know what the intent is. Just keep that in mind," she said.

He said, "Good. I think I can do that." Then he closed his notebook and pulled the wrapped package out of his backpack. It was oddly shaped. He said, "This is a present for you for the holidays and for mentoring me. I thought of you when I saw it."

Surprised, she carefully unwrapped it. Inside was a woodcarving of three dolphins moving gracefully through water. Her eyes lit up immediately. "This is beautiful, Jeremy! Thank you so much."

"You're welcome. I can't tell you what your mentoring has meant to me," he said with a warm smile. "I know I wouldn't be where I am without you."

"You're more than welcome, Jeremy. It's been great for me, and I don't really expect this to end. Know what I mean?" she asked. Then, with a mischievous smile, she said, "You know I'll be calling you too at some point to ask you to mentor a new manager. Take another new manager under your wing. You can pay me back by paying it forward."

"Agreed," he said. "I'd love to."

Glancing at the counter, she said, "Well, I guess I've got to go. Happy New Year, Jeremy!"

They hugged, and he headed home to Sasha.

Start the Next Year by Looking at the Last Year

Jeremy had formulated a plan for a staff offsite the second Friday in January when they were all back from the holiday break. Ken had approved funding for it, and his staff was excited about the prospect of another trip to Grand Lakes Resort. Other than the location detail, Jeremy told them that it was intended to prepare the team for the next year. When pressed for details, he just smiled and said they didn't have to do any pre-work to prepare.

He also told them that Ken had given Jeremy a $2,000 team award for manufacturing's contributions toward All Pro's success last year. He asked what ideas they had for using it.

"How about we celebrate by having dinner together after the offsite and invite our partners?" Gia asked.

Jeremy said, "Good idea. Our significant others put up with a lot of angst over the last year."

The team gathered again at Grand Lake Resort on Friday, January 12. They started the offsite with a breakfast together overlooking the lake before moving into the conference room. Jeremy had already posted copies of their values, vision, and norms on the wall.

"We're going to review this last year by creating our team story over the last thirteen months. Bradley, could you help me hang this up?" Jeremy pulled out a long roll of blank paper, and they taped it to the wall. It stretched across the entire length of it.

Jeremy had already written "13 Months Ago . . ." in the far left corner. At the other end, their vision was circled inside of a sun. Jeremy had also carefully written each month from the year along the bottom of the paper. The team was curious.

"We're going to document our entire year, in our own words." Jeremy wrote "People, Events, Results" along the left side. "This will be our team story for the last year. We can see where we came from, where we went, and how we got here all on one very large piece of paper," Jeremy explained. "I want to capture everything that happened this last year and what we learned through our own eyes." Jeremy put a pack of colorful markers on the table and took the black one.

"So, what should we say about where we started at the beginning of the year?" Jeremy asked.

The table was quiet, something Jeremy didn't expect. Anya let out a short laugh and ducked her head, as if she had to physically keep words from coming out of her mouth. It wasn't like her.

"Just say it," Bradley said, giving her a knowing look. Their relationship had vastly improved after their blowup over the adhesive.

"Well, I don't know if I should," she said, now with a serious look on her face.

"Go ahead," Jeremy said.

"Well, we were talking about how bad things were." She was looking at Gia.

Jeremy saw Gia thinking about what she might have talked to Anya about thirteen months ago. Then, she got a panicked look on her face and said, "Oh." Stammering, she said, "I'm not sure about sharing that." She was looking at Anya intently.

"Spill it," said Charlie.

"Well, we were talking about our previous manufacturing managers and how bad they'd been. Then . . ." and she paused again.

"You wondered how they'd come up with me as the next one," Jeremy said with a laugh. "I completely understand. I'd never been a manager before and never worked in production. Once I got over the glow from the promotion, I felt the same way." Then, he took a red marker and said, "Let me draw myself in." He drew a stick figure with bulging eyes and a question mark above it.

He laughed, looked around, and said, "I'm sure you're not the only ones." He was looking at Charlie and Bradley.

Bradley said, "Guilty as charged."

"Okay, for that, each of you has to draw yourself up here," Jeremy said, handing out markers to everyone.

They did. Most were just slightly better than Jeremy's. Gia had an artistic side they didn't know about, and her figure was the most recognizable.

That loosened everyone up.

Jeremy then drew a phone above January of last year. He said he drew it because the call from Ben at Symmetry had put him in a deep hole of angst when Ben had threatened to pull their business from All Pro. Then he drew another figure next to the phone.

"Who's that?" Gia asked.

"This is when I met a very important person who had a big impact on me this last year," Jeremy said. He turned to the group and told them about his first meeting with Josephine. He explained that, yes, she was the owner of Roast and also *the* Josephine, the founder of Brilliant Tech. Several got her name right away, but he had to explain to Gia and Aaron that she'd been a legend in Silicon Valley because of her teams and business results as an executive at several high-tech companies.

He told them she'd been his mentor through the last year and was really responsible for many of the surprises he'd thrown at them, such as clarifying role responsibilities. They were amazed.

"That explains it," Anya said. "She's well known for the fact that her employees loved working for her." She paused. "I see that now," she said with a knowing look on her face. Others nodded.

"What did she teach you?" Gia asked.

Turning toward the map, Jeremy wrote the five steps above the map at about the point when he implemented them with the team. "Step 5: Renewal," he wrote above "January," the current month. Jeremy briefly described the steps and what he did. He said, "I'll add more in as we go from the Five Steps, but let's talk about what happened at the beginning."

Charlie jumped in. "Back in March, Bradley and I were talking about the Symmetry ultimatum and the goals we needed to hit. We agreed: we're screwed!"

"We couldn't hit any of those goals," Bradley added. Everyone laughed, including Jeremy. He had Charlie depict that on their story. He drew a screw inside a dark cloud above March.

Aaron jumped up and grabbed a marker. He picked a red one and drew a cartoon of himself above April, buried beneath a pile of papers with one arm reaching up into the air. Everyone laughed. He explained he had felt buried by all the spreadsheets he had to fix.

Aaron's drawing reminded everyone of how they had felt at different times during the year. They began moving through the year, month by month. They each took a different colored marker and took turns adding events, crucial meetings, and people. A picture of the sales manager smiling and shaking hands with Aaron in July marked

Aaron's acceptance into the order forecast meetings with sales and marketing. Jeremy made sure they added their setbacks as well as their accomplishments.

Jeremy depicted his meetings with Ken, especially when he was asking for funding. He encouraged his team to add their own. Anya added a picture of her hair coming out after talking to the adhesive supplier in August. Bradley added his own picture with his eyes bulging out when he found out that the sensor was indeed broken and he'd accused Anya of not doing her job. They laughed. Everyone had his or her own events, both good and bad.

They included their team metrics and actual results. Q2's bad results were written inside a storm cloud with lightning. Q4's results were proudly written inside a sun. Business happenings took up most of the paper. The team was having fun creating the map; no one was sitting down, and they reminisced about the good happenings and even had a few conversations about how to ensure certain setbacks wouldn't happen next year.

The team shared a lot of backstories the others hadn't known. Charlie recounted a lunch meeting with a customer where he insisted they pick the restaurant and found himself at a barbecue with a menu full of only beef and chicken meals. Charlie was a vegetarian.

The map filled up quickly, and they reached the sun with their inscribed vision before they knew it. They all stepped back to admire their work. It was a healthy mix of colors, words, pictures, and graphs.

"Can we hang this up in the office?" Anya asked.

"It shouldn't go to waste. It's a fine piece of artwork," Jeremy said, thinking it would be a good morale booster for the next year, which could be even busier than the last year had been.

Learning from the Past and Celebrating Success

They took a break with a leisurely lunch on the sunny patio.

When they regrouped in the conference room, Jeremy said, "Let's capture learnings we want to carry into the next year. This next year could be even busier. We'll have to at least maintain our team metrics and dramatically increase our volume."

He said, "I want you to think about this last year. Then I want us to break into pairs and brainstorm what we think the team should continue to do, start doing, or stop doing. We'll take thirty minutes to do that, and you can go anywhere on site here." He handed out sticky notes and asked them to put one start, stop, or continue per sticky note.

The energy level was high, and they were all still going after thirty minutes. Jeremy gave them an extra five.

Jeremy, with Aaron's help, put up three sheets, START, STOP, and CONTINUE, and posted them on the wall. Then he had each pair talk about theirs and put them up on the sheets under the right heading. The CONTINUE sheet had, by far, the most notes. START had just a few, and STOP had just one.

They discussed the CONTINUE list and what seemed to have the most impact. The first was Jeremy's unrelenting focus on the vision, team norms, team metrics, and team strategies. Gia summed it up when she said, "We all knew what was important and that we were all accountable."

Charlie chimed in. "We all contributed even if something wasn't necessarily in our area because of that accountability. And the fact that Jeremy wanted our ideas helped too."

"The positivity on the team was almost as important," Bradley said. Jeremy was surprised that that comment had come from Bradley. Bradley must have realized they hadn't expected him to say that. "I know that I can live in the dark side, the negative side," he explained. Looking at Jeremy, he said, "You kept things pretty positive even when things weren't going so well. And others chipped in too. I needed to hear that, and, though it may not have looked like it, it worked."

"I saw it," Anya said. "You keep us grounded in what can go wrong." She paused before saying, "And sometimes things do go wrong." They both laughed.

As they discussed the CONTINUE list, Jeremy got a little lost in the discussion. He was thinking about how the Five Steps had really made a difference.

It was Gia who got his attention. "Jeremy, you there?"

He realized he'd been daydreaming. She asked, "Did you hear what I asked about job rotations? On the START sheet. I'd like to see if we could have some job shadowing in other areas. Like, I want to learn more about production, and Charlie might want to learn more about procurement." Charlie nodded in agreement.

Jeremy refocused and said, "That sounds good to me as long as you coordinate with each other. I think that'd be good for the business."

They looked at the one sticky on the STOP list. It said "three-hour staff meetings." "That was mine," Charlie said. "Having the same three agenda items was really important. It's just the meetings are so long."

Jeremy looked around and saw several nods. He said, "They are long, but we have so much to get through." He saw Charlie nod in agreement. Jeremy continued, "But hopefully, things won't be quite so chaotic. Let's cut them back to two hours. If we find that's not enough, I'll bump them up again."

He looked around the group and at the START, STOP, and CONTINUE sheets and asked, "Anything else for the group from these?" Hearing nothing, he said, "Let's take a break, and we'll get back together in fifteen minutes."

Individual Assessments

When they returned, Jeremy said, "I want to have each of us take an hour and think about our own accomplishments, our own growth this last year, and what we want to START, STOP, and CONTINUE this next year." He handed out a form and said, "You can use this if you want or come up with your own." He paused and then said, "I know performance reviews are due at the end of January." He heard several groans. "I've never written one, and I'm not planning to write yours."

"What?" Anya said with surprise in her voice. Then she got it. She smiled and said, "I know. You want us to write them. Is that Josephine's idea?"

He laughed and said, "Yes, but I completely get it. I'm going to write mine, so if I can write mine, you can write yours." He thought he saw Charlie about to protest. He quickly said, "This exercise will help. For your performance review, document your many accomplishments, your strengths, and what you want to focus on this next year. I'll give you my input."

They each found an area to work on their own.

Jeremy listed his accomplishments. He documented both business results and team results. He was almost more proud of the team's results than the business results. He had a long list of things he wanted to continue, a few on the STOP list, and more than a few on the START list. He'd been so internally focused within manufacturing. He knew he needed to shift more of his time and energy outside manufacturing, with customers and peers. He could delegate more to his staff.

He was just about finished when Gia walked up. "Do you have a minute?" she asked.

He said, "Sure. How's this exercise working for you?"

"It's working really well. In fact, it's made me think about looking outside manufacturing and into other areas. Marketing maybe. I wanted to get your thoughts, though."

Jeremy sighed. He realized she'd seen him, and she looked disappointed. He didn't want her to misunderstand, so he quickly responded, "No, I didn't handle that very well, did I? You're really good, and I wouldn't want to lose you. But I'd support your move if that's what you want. In fact, I can talk to Leo, the marketing VP, if you want."

She broke into a big smile. "You would? That'd be awesome. It probably won't happen right away. I don't know if they have any openings. I just thought about it today."

He said, "Just let me know." Gia walked away with a smile. He thought, I hope that's not just the start. Everyone finished their form. He thought he saw looks of satisfaction on everyone's faces.

The team members regrouped in the bar area before dinner. They were all seated around a table. After the waiter had taken their orders, Jeremy said, "There's one more thing I need to tell you about." He paused, looking around. "Richard and Ken have asked us to present the past year's results as a team to the two of them." The direct reports exchanged glances.

"No pressure," Anya said.

"I think it'll be a good meeting," Jeremy said with an encouraging tone. "We have great results. I want each of you to have the opportunity to present what you've accomplished." The team members seemed nervous, but they agreed they'd like the opportunity.

Shortly after, everyone's significant other arrived for dinner. Jeremy and each team member introduced their partners as the resort staff served drinks and appetizers. After they were seated and had placed their dinner orders, Jeremy proposed a toast with special champagne Sasha had brought. He thanked each of the partners by name for their patience and support over the last year.

"We couldn't have gotten through this last year without your support. Thank you so much," Jeremy said. He was looking directly at Sasha by that point. They had a wonderful dinner.

Sharing Lessons Learned

The week had gone by quickly, and soon the team was back in the conference room, but with two visitors, Richard and Ken. Jeremy opened the meeting but structured the agenda so most of the time and focus would be on his direct reports and what they'd accomplished.

"We didn't just magically get where we are now," Jeremy started. "It was a year-long process, and everyone in this room worked long and hard to get us here. And we're still learning." Jeremy displayed the team mission and vision on the projector.

"We learned a lot about what it takes to build the trust and commitment of a high-performance team. We keep going back to our fundamentals." Jeremy walked through the mission, vision, and team rules. He explained how they used them in their staff meetings.

After that, he invited Richard and Ken to join him in front of the team map they had taped to the wall. The team jumped in to walk them through the history map.

Richard enjoyed the map. The CEO laughed at the pictures and started taking notes. Jeremy took it as a good sign. Ken and Richard were surprised when Jeremy shared that *the* Josephine had been his mentor through the year. They commented on her amazing reputation.

"You're a smart manager to listen to her," Richard commented. He asked questions about different events. Jeremy made sure to thank Ken for funding their strategy work after he apologized for his stick figure drawing of Ken on the map. Ken laughed and said, "Well, I didn't hire you to be an artist, that's for sure."

Bradley walked them through the START, STOP, and CONTINUE sheets with the yellow sticky notes still attached from the offsite. Richard concluded, "You're doing a lot of things right, it looks like. Maybe there's something here we could learn from." He was looking at Ken, who nodded in agreement.

Next, Jeremy had Aaron show them the team scorecard. He'd summarized it for the entire year by quarter with the green, yellow, and red dots. "You have a great trend going," Richard said. "Can you keep it up this year?"

Jeremy looked around at his team and said, "We think we can. We've learned so much. Some of it the hard way."

Then, Jeremy's staff members individually presented details on the team goals and strategies for the year and how they'd achieved them by the end of Q4. Richard and Ken listened and asked questions throughout. Richard was especially intrigued by their decision to redefine their own role with their largest customers from just being a supplier to being a trusted partner.

Bradley offered, "That was Anya's idea."

Richard said, "Brilliant."

Anya beamed.

Everyone had the opportunity to demonstrate what they'd accomplished. Jeremy was quiet throughout the presentations, realizing how fortunate he was to have these people on his team and to witness their growth over the year. A year ago, Aaron wasn't even on the team, and the rest of his staff wouldn't talk to each other. He wouldn't have believed it if someone had told him then that this was the same team.

By the time the presentation was finished, Ken had a hefty amount of notes, and he asked Jeremy to forward everything they'd reviewed except, of course, the team story. He could always visit the manufacturing conference room, where it was taped to the wall. Jeremy was about to stand up to wrap up the presentation when Anya stood.

"We have one more thing we would like to present," she said. Jeremy was surprised. They hadn't planned anything else.

"Of course," Jeremy said, sitting back down in his seat. Ken looked at him, then at Anya and Bradley, who were approaching the front of the room. Anya connected her laptop to the projection system, and a presentation titled "Our High-Performance Team" came up.

Jeremy was nervous. But as soon as Anya started talking, he realized he had no reason to be.

"We've vastly improved as a department and a team over this past year," she began. "None of it would have happened if Jeremy hadn't invested his time and effort into getting us to this point."

"We talked about and created this presentation as a team," Bradley said. "We agreed Jeremy's approach was the single most important reason we achieved what we did."

"We've established six areas in which Jeremy excelled." Anya took over again, clicking through the slides on her laptop.

"First, Jeremy was honest and authentic with us throughout the entire process. He explained what he was doing and why and admitted when he didn't know how to do something and was overwhelmed. He didn't sugarcoat our department's position with our customers or within All Pro. He was transparent in everything he did."

Bradley talked while Anya changed the slides. "Second, he got the right people on our team and set us up for success. We had a weak link on our team, and Jeremy dealt with that. He then hired Aaron, who's done a fantastic job in such a short time.

"A third thing Jeremy did was invest time in building personal relationships and trust with us, as well as building trust within the team. That got us through some tough times."

Anya presented the final three points. "Jeremy focused on immediate and positive feedback. When he liked something, he let us know right away. It was encouraging and made it easier to bring up any issue to him. In that vein, a fifth thing Jeremy did was hold us accountable for our metrics and living the team rules. Even when we faltered"—Anya shared a look with Bradley—"he got us right back on track instead of freaking out and telling us we were failing. The final thing Jeremy did was to involve us in the business and the team's success. He let us give input, ideas, and opinions on what we should do to be successful. It created an environment where we felt valued."

Jeremy was reeling with the unexpected praise.

"Thank you, all of you, truly," Jeremy said, at a loss for words. "This team is the best."

Richard was looking at Ken. "Thank you for the presentation and again for all of your hard work. Ken, would you mind stepping outside with me for a minute?" Richard asked. He and Ken stood up from the table.

"Did we just epically fail?" Aaron whispered as soon as they left. Everyone shook their heads or shrugged. Jeremy's heart was pounding. He was certain the presentation went well. They didn't have to wait long before Ken and Richard returned.

"I couldn't be more pleased with your results," Richard said as they stood at the end of the table. "You've created a solid competitive advantage for us as a company. Because of you, we're going to grow next year. I'm already getting calls from customers who want to expand production with us. I'm even getting calls from new customers. They want a company they can depend on." He paused a moment before continuing. "Ken and I had been planning to talk to Jeremy in private, but now seems as good a time as ever." He stepped back and let Ken take the spotlight.

"It hasn't been announced yet, but I am retiring at the end of this July. And I'm naming Jeremy as my successor as chief operation officer, if he accepts," Ken said. The room was stunned into silence, especially Jeremy. He tried to digest what was happening.

Ken explained, "The transition won't be complete until the end of the year. You'll have all of my responsibilities, as well as a second job helping Richard implement your practices company wide."

Jeremy said nothing. Words had left him. Everyone was looking at him.

"Well?" Anya said. Everyone laughed, Jeremy included. She brought Jeremy back to the moment, and he stood up.

"I'd love to. Thank you for your faith in me."

Performance Reviews

Over the next several weeks, Jeremy met with each direct report to go over the performance review they'd written and to discuss the reorganization they were going through as part of Jeremy's promotion. Instead of going through a hiring process for a new manager, Jeremy offered the position to Bradley, who accepted. He told Jeremy he felt he could succeed after what he'd learned in the last year, and because Jeremy would still be his manager. Bradley suggested Anya become production manager. Anya was surprised but excited about the prospect. Anya asked Jeremy to see if Josephine could make time to meet with her and Gia. They wanted to talk to her about her experience in managing and leading teams as a woman in high tech. He promised to check.

Charlie wanted to continue in his quality role and go after his certification. Gia was moving to marketing and was thrilled about becoming a product manager. Aaron would continue as the planner for the group, but he would expand his responsibilities with more direct meetings with customers.

"Your continued work will set you up for a move into any of the other functions within manufacturing," Jeremy told Aaron, who said he was looking forward to his new focus on external relationships.

Next Steps and Challenges for Jeremy

Jeremy met Josephine late in the afternoon on Thursday, February 1. She ushered him to their usual table with his coffee and her tea mug. He told her of his promotion, and she beamed.

"Congratulations! And, you've completed the Five Steps in just about a year's time frame," she said. "Well, you're not completely done."

Jeremy looked at her, perplexed. "There's more?" he asked.

"Always," she replied. "You've completed your first cycle. Now you get to start a new one, with your new role. A new position with new challenges and new people." She told him being a COO was one of the most rewarding positions she'd ever held.

"What are you going to do now?" she asked as he hugged her good-bye.

"I'm going to go home and tell Sasha," he said.

"She might have a surprise for you too," Josephine said with a smile.

Jeremy went straight home. Josephine's comment puzzled him, but he was eager to share his news.

"Hey, I didn't know you'd be home early," Sasha said when he arrived. He beamed and told her about the meeting and his promotion.

"That's wonderful," she said. "I'm so proud. What a difference a year makes."

"Josephine said you have a surprise for me?" Jeremy asked.

"Yes I do. I'm pregnant," Sasha said, smiling slowly.

Jeremy wasn't ready for the news, and it took a second to process. Then he laughed and picked her up, twirling her around. She staggered when he set her on her feet.

"Whoops, are you okay?"

"Of course." Sasha was laughing. "Does this mean you're happy?"

"I couldn't be happier," Jeremy said. Jeremy already loved his happy, new challenges.

MORE ABOUT THE FIVE-STEP MODEL

In my work with numerous leaders and managers, it has become obvious to me that managers who intentionally build and sustain high-performance teams over time are more successful. Almost every one completes an assessment of him- or herself and his or her team to understand what needs to be done to take the team to the next level. And getting to the next level is a business necessity.

Using the following model, you can start at step 1 and go through each step in order. If you've already done all five steps, you may realize you need to go back and focus more on one particular step. Your most critical action, though, is to actively use the model.

The following is the complete model followed by a short summary of each step:

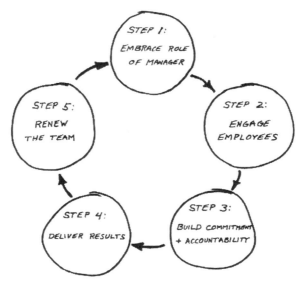

Step 1 is "Embrace Your Role as a Manager." The role of a manager is challenging as you have to make sure you achieve your business goals while also managing a group of individuals. It's imperative in this step to assess your transition into the role and what is working or not working well. One of the biggest challenges is that the basic nature of your work has probably changed. As an individual contributor, you did the work. Now, as a manager, you have to get work done through others. You don't directly control your employees. They will do their best work for you and the organization when they have a trusting and effective relationship with you.

It's key in this step to understand your own personality and work preferences, including your strengths and weaknesses. You can then adapt your behavior to form more positive and effective relationships with your employees. You may already have a good understanding of your own interpersonal style and strengths and weaknesses. An assessment such as DISC or MBTI can also be useful in this step. I recommend you share personal insights on your preferences in how you work and your strengths and weaknesses. This will open the door to productive discussions with your team and employees on how you can work most effectively together. This will build trust with your employees. Trust is the foundation for your success and sets you up to successfully go on to Step 2

Step 2, "Engage Employees," starts with ensuring your team is structured for success and that you have the right employees on the team. You may need to deal with employees who are a poor fit for their role or for the team. If hiring, you will need to make a great hire, and you'll use a performance-based hiring process to improve the quality of your hire. It's important in this step to ensure every employee documents his or her responsibilities, if possible, and the results he or she is expected to achieve. Employees should share their position profiles with each other so it's clear who is responsible for what. You may need to ensure clarity on any gray areas where employees share portions of a process or product.

Once employees document their responsibilities, you will discuss those responsibilities and expected results with each employee to ensure alignment. You and your employee will agree on the support you'll provide so the employee is successful.

Step 3 is "Build Commitment and Accountability to the Team and the Business." As in Step 1, a team must have trust among its members in order to have commitment and accountability. People tend to trust other people when they get to know them. You'll create opportunities for employees to get to know each other by providing an opportunity to share personal information and also information about their work preferences. You and your team will develop team rules or norms in how everyone interacts with each other and the team.

To build commitment to the business, you will lead the team in developing or, at least, discussing the mission, vision, and goals of the team. It's critical that you provide employees with the opportunity to provide input. In addition, the team will discuss and develop team strategies to accomplish the goals of the team. You'll gain the benefit of getting everyone's ideas, and you'll get better solutions. Employees will determine what part of the goals and team strategy they own, and they'll develop their own SMART goals that cascade from the team's goals. This will drive accountability for results.

Step 4, "Deliver Results," focuses on managing the team's performance so the team achieves its goals. You will lead your team to define and develop a short list of team metrics that measure whether the team is successful. You will set up a review process to make sure you are on track to hit your metrics and implement your strategies as needed for success. You and the team will meet on a regular basis to review your progress, and you'll make course corrections as needed. Feedback, for both the team and employees, is critical in this step. You'll understand why you need to emphasize ongoing and positive feedback so your team stays motivated and energized. You'll understand the steps in providing effective feedback.

Step 5 is "Renewal." It is critical for any team or employee to periodically pause and assess the past, the present, and the future. This provides both you and the team a needed break from your regular routine and an opportunity to celebrate successes and growth. This starts by understanding what has transpired to get the team or employee to the present. It's extremely helpful to capture learnings from the past and celebrate successes and growth. This will yield critical information for reviews and development planning. It's also provides a springboard to a successful start of your next cycle or project.

Nothing ever stays the same. Change is ongoing. You change, your employees change, customers and competitors change. You can repeatedly use this model to ensure you and your team are set up for success over the long term.

I hope you find this book and model useful. You can find more information on our website, *TeamBuildingforSuccess.com*, about the resources we offer, including coaching and development programs to complete the 5 steps with your team.

ACKNOWLEDGEMENTS

This book has had many contributors. I would like to acknowledge those people. First, to my husband Stan, for his ongoing support. I appreciate his willingness to read several drafts of the book and his invaluable feedback. Second, I'd like to thank my two children, Ryan and Sarah, for their encouragement and ongoing support. And Sarah, thanks for listening to me read my manuscript to you on our drive to Colorado and then your editing. You have a great eye for writing.

I want to acknowledge the great work of my ghostwriter, Chelsea Hansen, who wrote much of the first draft and helped bring the characters and situations to life in the story. You have a gift for creating compelling scenarios.

Next, I offer my gratitude to Helen, Kristine and the staff at Author Bridge Media for guiding me through the book creation process. You patiently helped me revise my book so that it's much more readable. And your editing and publishing services have been wonderful.

I'd like to thank my friends and colleagues who gave me their support as I wrote the book and their feedback for the title, subtitle and book cover. I highly value your support and friendship.

Finally, I'd like to thank the many leaders and managers I've worked with over the years who 'intentionally' built great teams. This is especially true for those HP managers and employees who practiced 'the HP way' and worked hard to ensure that their businesses were successful. You really showed me how to balance both the head and the heart for the benefit of the company and the employees.

ABOUT THE AUTHOR

Donna Evans is the founder of Team Building for Success, a training and consulting company focused on creating a competitive advantage for it's clients through engaged employees and high performing teams. As a consultant, trainer and speaker, Donna works with leaders and managers in organizations to improve their bottom-line performance by harnessing the power of all of their employees.

Donna's interest in employee engagement and building great teams started with her first job in high school, packing processed meats at Bunny Brands Meat Packing in Townville, Pennsylvania. Following that adventure, Donna has worked at a number of organizations and companies and had the opportunities to be part of, study and lead a wide variety of work teams. Most notably was her employment at Hewlett-Packard working first as a financial analyst and then moving into human resources, where she was the HR manager for global and regional business teams.

While at HP, Donna became grounded in the HP Way as well as HP's ongoing business management processes. She worked with business leaders and managers to quickly form high performing teams to deliver tremendous business results and manage change.

Donna holds a B.S. in Pre-Medicine from Pennsylvania State University and an M.S. in Management from Purdue University. Donna lives in Poway, California with her husband, and two dogs. You can visit her blogs on leadership topics and best management practices at **www.teambuildingforsuccess.com**.

Lightning Source UK Ltd.
Milton Keynes UK
UKOW02f1905120117

291976UK00011B/153/P

9 780996 972802